It's Not Impossible: Healing from Ritual Abuse and Mind Control

For with men this is impossible, but with God all things are possible. Matthew 19:26

This book is dedicated to:

- The God of all love, mercy and forgiveness. He is good beyond belief, and the reason this book is possible.
- My daughter, Hoji. You bless me so much and I thank God for your courage and faith.
- Jo: You are a general in God's army, and a lover of all that is good. Thank you for showing what Christian love is like.
- Cheri: When you pray, God answers, because you are His friend. Thank you.
- T: You were there during some of the hardest parts of the journey, and showed unfailing faith and courage.
- My children and loved ones still in the cult: I pray for you daily, for your freedom.

Contents

Introduction

This is a book about healing from some of the most difficult traumas a human being can undergo. I wrote the book for one purpose: to help those on the journey realize it is possible to heal and to help those supporting them understand what they are trying to heal from.

I have been on my own healing journey for 27 years. It started when I went for deliverance years ago, and continued during the time when I realized that I was a member of a satanic cult, chose to leave the group, was abused and tortured and forced to recant, and then by God's grace chose to continue to heal from *those* traumas. I wrote numerous articles that have been published on the Internet and shared with others earlier in this healing journey. Those articles reflected my understanding of healing at that time. This book reflects my understanding in the years since, after numerous access attempts (some successful, many not), and a deepening walk with God, who is my true healer.

I used to be a programmer for a group that stands behind the Illuminati, Knights Templar, Opus Dei, Magnificat, Trinity and the other international occultic organizations (there are twelve in all). In fact, I used to be their head programmer, and ran the programming labs for this organization after Mengele died, when the torch was first passed on to another, and then to me. I developed or helped develop many of the programs discussed in this book or "improved" on those developed before my time. I no longer work for that group, and this book is my restitution. My other restitution is this: I pray that all who were ever programmed by me, or with the technologies that I developed, will be freed and released, in the name of the true Jesus who heals and blesses and forgives. I am forgiven for all that I did, by a God who shows amazing grace and mercy. He has literally held me as I shook and cried and screamed at times, both during the actual traumas, and during the healing of them. He has never left my side, throughout the journey. He never abandons during the journey, even though it can be difficult at times.

Many will ask "Where did you go during the years you disappeared?" I chose to go offline, had no cell phone, and lived with a safe friend during the five years of that part of my healing. I was then tested greatly, and found that God would come through. During this time, one my daughters (Hoji) chose to leave the group as well, in large part due to my testimony for Christ. She remembers (as I do, as well) being there when I was tortured for my faith in Christ, and that I whispered "I forgive you" to her and the others present (leaders of this organization). With this I want to add: "I want you to get free" to each of my loved ones who are still in the group. It really is possible to get free, and this book is my testimony to this fact. May it help and bless those who read its pages.

svali

Chapter One: Essentials to Deprogramming (What Needs to Be in Place Before Starting)

Healing from mind control programming is possible, but it is not easy. One of the most difficult issues that therapists and supporters face is the heartbreak of seeing individuals that they attempt to help break free get accessed continuously while the individual is completely unaware. They must weigh the attempt to help against the possibility of harm, since attempts to heal can be used against the survivor if they are accessed.

Before attempting to heal from occultic programming, it is important to have support in place if at all possible. This is difficult work and having the support that is needed can make a huge difference in success and preventing reaccess. Below are suggestions for finding support.

Safe Support and accountability

First and foremost, it is important to have a safe support person in your life who can provide accountability (i.e. help ensure that you aren't doing missions overseas for three months when you thought you were going to college or working). You will want to have someone you can talk to, vent to, or let your parts out around who will not be a perpetrator to you or them. There are numerous reasons for needing support during healing, but the foundational reason is this: the wounding to the survivor was done relationally, and healing is also done relationally (i.e. the survivor was hurt by people, and the survivor needs people to heal).

I have heard of survivors (with government mind control, not extensive occultic programming) who have been able to heal "solo" but this is extremely rare. While the individual may be able to break programming and become free of access, these individuals may integrate, but do not truly heal, because there has not been the healthy attachment or modeling of healthy behavior that is needed for true relational healing.

Finding safe support may sound simple, but safe support and accountability from a non-dissociative person can be extremely hard to find.

Why is this? One reason is that most programmed survivors will be almost literally surrounded by cult people; and early in their therapy, they will have no idea that this is so. The loving husband who supports your therapy and drives you to sessions may actually be a handler (this was true for me, of my first two husbands). The best friend who is "always there" for you may be a cult sister. Family members are often also members of the group a survivor is trying to leave.

I have had many survivors ask me "If I was in the cult, is it possible that my husband wasn't?" My heart breaks when I hear this question, because almost always, the answer is "no." People who grew up in a cult group that programmed them will not be allowed to choose their own spouse; the cult chooses them.

What about people who "got away" from the group in their teens?

This is another question I have been asked frequently. The history often goes like this:

the survivor remembers being part of a cult group in their early childhood, then believes that they somehow "escaped" when they left home to go to college or got married. In most cases, the belief that the survivor "left" is a cover memory, designed to cover the fact they are still active and doing their cult jobs. Most cult groups have put time and effort into programming members and do not simply let people "leave". I have also heard many stories of survivors who later in therapy realized that they never did leave, and the husband or partner they "chose" is actually their handler (an individual whose job is to watch them, report on them, and ensure that they are doing their cult jobs).

Another reason it is extremely difficult to find safe support and accountability is the lack of education and unwillingness in the church to provide these things to survivors. This is not a "slam" against churches, but the reality: many survivors report negative experiences if they disclose the fact that they are breaking free from a cult to their church. This can be due to several reasons:

- People in the church don't understand their authority in Christ, and are afraid of the spiritual warfare that they believe a survivor will bring into the church if they help the survivor

- The church has had previous bad experiences with infiltrators who had jobs of promoting negative perceptions of survivors and creating chaos, division or burnout within the church

- Misunderstanding within the church regarding the need for support and accountability. A survivor may be erroneously seen as "paranoid" or "not trusting God with their safety." Requests for accountability are misunderstood due to ignorance in the church about how cults work or how access occurs

- Fear of the cult and fear of possible physical retaliation. This fear is reinforced by some very bad teaching about cults and survivors

Realistically, when looking for support and accountability, the survivor may not have many – if any - options. There are very few "safe houses" (and most that do exist have been reported to be infiltrated). Early in their journey, the survivor will want to pray that God does provide this accountability and support.

Ideally, a support person will have the following characteristics:

- **They are not dissociative**, or are a **completely** healed survivor. This requires discernment because it is not uncommon for "supporters" or those in prayer ministries who are drawn to work with survivors to be dissociative, and completely unaware of this fact. I have heard of numerous accounts of a survivor's "support person" learning that they themselves are dissociative, and neither they nor the survivor initially suspected this fact. Survivors should be especially wary of individuals that they feel an "instant connection with" (real friendship takes time). Also, some "integrated" survivors later discover that only the top levels of their systems joined, while deeper levels continued to be cult active. Get to know a person well, and be prayerful, before asking them into a support role.

- **Mature.** All too often, supporters of survivors have their own unhealed wounds that can negatively impact the survivor. I have heard numerous horror stories of survivors who worked almost as slaves in return for a room in a house; or of emotional abuse (including Christian abuse) in which the survivor was berated for "taking so long to heal" or "not having the faith to integrate quickly" by individuals who did not understand how mind control works or what the process of healing looks like. This can be extremely damaging to a survivor who is already struggling with antichristian programming.

- **Have a strong faith.** While I have known survivors who worked on healing without Christianity, I personally cannot imagine healing occultic abuse and the demonic oppression that results without going to the real source of healing: the loving God who created us and never abandoned us, even during the worst of the abuse. Anyone who supports survivors of ritual abuse must have a source of strength, joy and spiritual refreshment to help them in the battle against the demonic, or they will burn out. It helps tremendously to help others from the viewpoint of victory; and the Holy Spirit can provide the wisdom, discernment and love that no other source can.

Therapist

During healing, it is also important to have a therapist who is knowledgeable and experienced in dealing with cult programming. Healing work involves coming in touch with deep trauma, including intense emotions and painful memories. A therapist who is warm, has faith that you can heal, and can help support you through this journey can make a huge difference.

Church

Another possible source of strength while healing and deprogramming is a **strong, loving church**. Some of the best help for healing – and some of the worst spiritual and verbal abuse – comes from churches, which makes it important to find one that is *helpful.*

Look for a church that is based upon the Bible, and where the people are accepting. People who shun or avoid you because you are a survivor will impede your healing. Does the church have a ministry that helps those recovering from emotional, spiritual or sexual abuse? You may not want to initially disclose that you are a survivor of cult abuse or mind control; instead, you may want to check out their ministry to other issues first.

About Safe Houses

Safe houses are a controversial topic, and for good reason. I lived in the home of an individual who was not dissociative for two years during an intense portion of my own healing journey. While I was not accessed due to 24/7 accountability (which was good) I did endure some verbal and emotional abuse from the woman whose house I lived in. I was expected to cook, clean, help out financially and spend eight hours a day, five days a week journaling as a requirement of staying there, or I would be asked to leave. I did journal and discovered a lot about my parts and their jobs during this time, but at great emotional cost. I am grateful, however, that I had safety during those two years, and do appreciate her allowing me to stay there during this very difficult portion of my journey.

I also stayed at a “safe house” in which I was accessed (by my daughter from another country, who came to live there soon after I entered the house). The house was not safe, because I myself was not yet safe (I was unaware of my deepest double binds, which made me vulnerable to access), and because the other survivors in the house were quite early in their own healing journeys, and so were all also vulnerable to access.

If you are able to stay with a truly safe, non-dissociative friend or pastor who opens their home to you, you are fortunate indeed. But these situations are rare. Some “safe houses” are actually designed to access others attempting to leave the cult, and any survivor who chooses this route should exercise discernment and caution.

Women's shelters can be a short-term option, but often cult groups will send in a member after the person attempting to escape (this happened to me three times). Also, some women's shelters are managed by cult personnel for this very reason. Others know that they are not trained to deal with those escaping cult abuse. So pray before seeking safety to help ensure that the situation you are entering into is truly safe.

It is possible to heal without having all four types of support described above; you may only find one, if any, sources of help in your healing journey. If you can find safe accountability, this is the most helpful as you begin healing.

Chapter Two: Why Programming Works

Mind control involves the installation of programs into a person. "Programming" is convincing a person (a part/personality/alter) that he or she have no choice but to perform a particular action, or hold to a particular belief. While it can be helpful to understand *what* programming is present, an important foundation for healing is to understand *why* it works. Modern programming is based upon extensive scientific research (by individuals such as B.F. Skinner, Milton Erikson, Mengele and those who followed in his footsteps) as well as the application of spiritual principles that basically "lock it in" after it is installed. In other words, modern programming is a combination of science and spirituality.

Most programming consists of the following components. The length and complexity of each will vary with the skills of the programmers (also known as "trainers" but who are in actuality *abusers*). The components include:

1. Agreement to installation of the program
2. Participation in a ritual before installation
3. Installation of behavior and beliefs (with concurrent psychological, physical or tech torture)
4. Concurrent installation of command codes and triggers
5. Participation in a ritual after the programming session (sealing ritual)
6. Post-programming bonding session, during which the individual is comforted, and young (infant and child) parts are rocked, held, given bottles of formula or breast fed, and rewarded for "doing well" during the session

Why do people agree to have programming installed?

This often surprises survivors, who initially believe that they were unwilling victims of evil people (which can also be true). The reality is, they are often the *willing* victims of programmers because they are thinking and acting due to a lifetime of the installation (indoctrination) of false beliefs. This agreement is usually not conscious, since **the individual has usually made agreements within their presentation to not remember their own programming**.

What kind of false beliefs bring a person to the point of allowing the installation of programming? In most groups, this programming begins in the womb, while the individual is still a fetus. Mengele was the first to truly demonstrate and document the effects of fetal trauma and its role in controlling the individual; over the years, others built upon his work. Today, extensive trauma (torture of the birth mother) carrying the fetus and of the fetus is considered a routine part of programming.

The reasons for prenatal torture are numerous. One of the main goals is to develop in the individual the concept that the world (which they have never truly interacted with yet) is an unsafe place, where bad things happen. Then, when the trainer tells the fetus, "God hates you, that is why you and your mother are being hurt" the fetus will believe this lie and incorporate it into their belief system. This creates a primal belief which causes the fetus (and the core throughout the individual's lifetime) to mistrust God: The individual believes "God is bad, and He does not protect me from pain."

This primal belief then leads the fetus to accept the following lies:

- I must protect myself (because God can't or won't)
- I must protect my mother

Unfortunately, the fetus is very tiny, and is not God (the only one who can truly protect). This creates a conflict: if God will not protect me and my birth mother, then how do I protect her?

The trainer will then offer the fetus a solution to this dilemma. They will ask the fetus to accept a demon which they tell the fetus will "protect" them from pain, or will stop their mother's pain. As soon as the fetus agrees (this agreement is monitored both by brain scans and spiritually by the trainer), the torture is stopped, and the demonic enters in.

The demonic will wrap itself around the core, and creates the first dissociation, or split, with the demonic delusion shielding the fetus from its own pain. Most importantly, the fetus has learned to take the role of "God" in protecting itself from the pain of prenatal torture.
This idolatry (being one's own messiah, and the birth mother's messiah) causes the construction of a stronghold of beliefs and lies that later in life cause the individual to agree to their own programming. As the fetus grows and is born, they will later learn to "rescue" people they love, such as brothers, sisters, beloved parents and primary trainers they have bonded with.

This belief that the individual is responsible for the welfare and continued existence of others they love is installed repetitively in the womb. Why? Because programming will not hold unless it is agreed with, either consciously or unconsciously. The individual will be taught in set ups that the people they love most will die if they do not keep their programming running, or allow its installation. A critical part of undoing programming is to look at how these foundational lies are installed (that only I can rescue myself and the people I love; God does not care, and won't), and the traumas that underlie the beliefs.

False Belief Number Two: God Is Weak

Because the Christian God is able to help a survivor heal, the belief is often installed repetitively in the womb that God is not only unwilling, but unable to help the fetus. Setups are done in which the fetus is raped in the womb (with specialized instruments that resemble miniature Q-tip swabs) which causes intense fetal distress (in fact, some fetuses actually curl up and die in the womb from the intense emotional and physical pain that this causes). The fetus may also have its digits (toes, fingers) cut off in the early months of life in the womb, since these will grow back when done during the early months. While the torture is occurring, setups are done in which a false "jesus" comes into the room, and either abuses the fetus, or wrings his hands, declaring "I'm sorry I can't help you" or even cries, saying he is afraid.

During these setups, the birth mother is also tortured, and the false "jesus" plays out this script with her. This is an important part of setting up early belief systems in the fetus. Since fetal brain waves automatically synchronize with those of the mother, the fetus often experiences emotions that correspond with what the birth mother experiences; her fear, mistrust and fear of a false jesus who rapes and tortures her will be communicated to the fetus, and build up the belief that the Christian God is evil – and too weak to help during painful circumstances.

Chapter 3: Accessing: Why it Occurs and How to Prevent It

Accessing is a serious issue for survivors, so serious, that I am choosing to devote one of the early chapters in this book to this topic. It is important for both survivors and therapists to understand what accessing is, and the steps they can take to prevent it from happening.

What is accessing?

Accessing is the deliberate contact of a survivor by the group (or affiliates) that they left, in order to intimidate and frighten parts into doing their cult jobs. Access may be as short and simple as a single sentence in an email that scares a part into shutting down therapy or withdrawing from healthy support. It can also be more complex, for instance, a survivor returning to a cult facility for hours for reprogramming.

If a person was raised in an organized group, they will have programming put in to make them accessible by the group. This is considered base-level programming to prevent their leaving.

How is accessing done?

Accessing is done by several methods, depending upon the stage of healing and awareness of the survivor.

One misconception people have is that accessing is done by mysterious, scary "bad" people who follow the survivor around and try to harm them when out and about. **But the number one person who accesses the survivor is the survivor themself**. They will have recontact programming installed that makes them become extremely anxious if they do not have regular contact with their cult handlers.

Cell phones are the number one method of accessing used by the cult. All survivors who have left an organized group will have programming in place to contact cult members by phone, or to receive messages or calls from cult members by phone. The survivor often will have absolutely no recollection that they received a text or message from the cult (this is how the amnesia linked to this programming works).

Who contacts the survivor? In most cases, the person's **immediate family** will be the members of the group chosen to contact the survivor. This could be a mother, father, aunt, uncle, brother, sister, children or grandchildren, or other family members. Texts back and forth about "family matters" will often have hidden messages or cues within them, reminding the person's cult parts of their jobs, and the programmed threat that goes with them.

- Examples: "Your family really loves you" is a frequent cue to cult-loyal parts to remember that only the cult can love them.

- "I love you and miss you" can be a cue that if the person does not re-contact, that the person's double binds will be put into danger, or tortured.

- "We haven't heard from you in a while" is an even stronger message that the person's cult parts need to contact, or someone they love will get hurt.

Often, cute videos of family members are sent as reinforcements of the fact that if the person tries to break free, or their parts stop doing their old jobs, the people in the video will be tortured. There may be subliminals in the background reinforcing this message on an unconscious level.

The person's cell phone bill will not show the more blatant or direct cult calls or texts, because there are special codes that can be entered in that ensure that the calls are not recorded by the phone company.

To break this re-contact programming, the individual's presentation (parts that live daily life, sometimes called host parts) need to show the programmed parts that **it is entirely possible to disobey the programming directives.** This involves breaking the program by:

1. Parts realizing there are options besides the directives
2. Parts giving up programmed lies for truth

The presentation parts may want to choose for a period of time to give up phone contact with cult-active associates or family members, until the person is sufficiently healed to be able to relate without being accessed.

If the person chooses to give up their cell phone (which should be done in order to break the programming, at least for a period of time), the group will then attempt to access the survivor by other methods. They will usually go to email or online next, since most people stay "connected" in these ways.

Emails with triggering subject lines from people the individual knows and trusts will appear around this time in healing. This is because most accessing occurs from people the person has known and loved most of their life. The individual has no idea that these members of their family, or church, or group of friends, is a cult member, since they will be amnesic to this fact until the parts begin coming forward and sharing information with them.

Subliminal Programming

Whenever a survivor uses technology such as a smart phone, goes online, plays video games, or watches current TV programs, they will be fed subliminal messages and images designed to fire off their NWO and other programming. These subliminals are part of Project Alexis, which was designed to prepare the world for the rise of the NWO. The images are fed at a speed of .03 microseconds (faster than conscious sight can see), with extremely rapid audios paired as well.

Once a survivor of cult programming signs into their email address, or visits Facebook, or signs into Amazon, or any other sites online, the subliminals linked to their profile will begin automatically feeding through their browser (there is no "safe" browser or operating system that can prevent this). Images of family members being hurt, and other distressing events, will be flashed by faster than the survivor can visually process. Ads with cues and triggers will also be displayed, and the individual may be completely unaware of this fact until they begin healing and working towards co-consciousness.

It becomes a "catch 22" in many ways: the emails, texts and subliminals frighten parts into not disclosing about family members, and the person is left wondering why their parts are not talking to them, or sharing much in therapy. The failure to disclose and amnesia keep the survivor in constant contact with cult members, while they are completely unaware of this fact. As a result, their cult parts continue to do their jobs, while the person's presentation has no idea that this is going on.

If a person chooses to give up their cell phone, and to go completely offline (or only limited online use with full accountability, i.e. someone watching while they check their bank statement, etc.) then the attempts to access by other methods will escalate.

Common forms of attempted access throughout the process of breaking free, and particularly at this point will include visual triggering by a visit from a family member if the individual is still in contact, or the cult placing someone who looks very similar to a double bind in view of the person. This could be a child who looks very much like a beloved child or grandchild standing next to the survivor at a store; or individuals who look just like a family member showing up when the survivor is in a public place. These are meant as nonverbal warnings: "If you don't obey us, this person will get hurt." These double bind lookalikes may also quickly sign messages to the survivor that they may be amnesic to (such as “help me” or “save me”) in order to trigger their recontact programming.

Cards by postal mail with threats may arrive; or voice mail messages with triggers may be left on a message machine. If the person has international presentations, mail addressed to the name of one of the other presenters, or a child or loved one from the other countries, may show up (i.e. "How odd, this mail came here and I don't know anyone by that name.")

Visual cues may be placed in the survivor's surroundings: a bouquet of flowers that has a special meaning; a special perfume on a card, or a 'gift" of a food that has a specific meaning to another presentation may appear.

If the individual cannot be accessed by other methods, the group will often attempt physical abduction. Often, the survivor will be taken somewhere by someone they know and trust, that they are unaware of as being a cult member, and physical accessing will then occur. If the survivor has too much co-consciousness to allow this, then physical threats and abuse may occur when the survivor is alone or in a vulnerable state.

Along with all of the above, the cult will also attempt spiritual access of the individual trying to break free. Dreams, threats and messages via astral projection may be given while sleeping, or even while awake, through demonic means. It is important that the individual prays about any open doors or parts with double binds that were programmed to stay in contact with loved ones who are cult members in this way.

Why is accessing done?

Accessing is done to make sure that the person's cult parts are continuing to do their jobs and that the presenters continue to remain clueless and amnesic. Continued access will cause continued amnesia and dissociation.

As mentioned previously, these jobs could include "internal", "spiritual" and "external"/"physical" jobs.

Internal jobs

- Making sure that the person's dissociation/amnesia is intact
- Protecting/guarding classified information or parts inside
- Blocking the person's healing
- Undoing the person's work in therapy
- Wearing out helpers
- Sending warfare and division internally and externally
- Participating in full rituals internally and calling on the demonic

External jobs

- Participating in rituals
- Active physical agendas against Christians and those helping survivors break free
- Sabotaging other survivors' safety or healing
- Assignments like research and assassinations
- Training of younger cult members
- Reporting to the cult
- Disseminating misinformation
- Discrediting other survivors and therapists

The person will normally be completely unaware that they have been triggered, or that their cult parts are doing their jobs, until later in healing.

Survivors commonly ask the following question regarding accessing:

If I pray, and ask that my Christian Host or presenters be present, could I still be accessed and unaware of the fact?

Yes. Why? Firstly, because the LORD does not set aside free will in the survivor, including the free will of parts who are still compliant with cult orders or who still want to protect loved ones in the cult way. Also, the Christian host, while a true believer, is often programmed to allow access and may have taken vows of amnesia and access, i.e. the Christian host/presentation is double-minded. Thirdly, the survivor often has a False Christian presentation that takes over the prayer that prays to a false "Jesus" or "God" before the Christian presenters (who pray to the true Christian God) have a chance to pray.

While the Christian presentation can pray, if other cult programmed parts that the Christian presentation is amnesic to rotate out due to a trigger or cue, the person can still be accessed and be completely unaware of this fact.

Here are two examples from real life. At one time, I took an accountability person (another survivor in therapy) with me each time I went to visit my children in another state (there was a custody battle, and at the time, I was only allowed supervised visitation with my children due to the risk of my abducting them in order to get them away from their abuse). Each time, my accountability person and I, as well as trusted church support members, would pray for my safety and ability to stay in my presentation and not lose time during the visitations.

Throughout the visits, I would pray continuously for safety with my accountability friend. On the way home, after each visit, I would thank the LORD with great relief for safety, and the fact that "nothing bad happened" during the visits, and gave praise reports to my church about how the LORD protected me and my friend, and answered our prayers for safety.

It wasn't until years later, and with more healing and deeper internal communication inside, and the amnesia dropping, that I discovered to my great distress that during each visit with my children, I had been accessed, tortured, and reprogrammed during the entire time. My accountability partner had been programmed to not remember these facts either. This is one reason why in general, other survivors do NOT make good accountability for a survivor.

The "safe visits" were actually cover memories that my Christian presentation was told to believe, or my children would be tortured and/or killed. Because I loved my children, there was a huge investment in not remembering, and so I had no idea of what actually happened during the visits. Memories of taking my children shopping were dealt with by cult members placing the items "purchased" in my car, and quick photos during the last hours of the visit were taken, with each photo staged to show different "fun activities" with my children.

In actuality, each visit was re-accessing and reprogramming by the cult, with orders given to not remember the accessing and to come again in several months. The amnesia at the time was complete, with absolutely no hint of what was actually occurring during the visits. My belief that the visits were safe, and that nothing bad had occurred, was real – and mistaken.

Another example:

One survivor who had broken off all contact with her family due to cult memories of them had a short meeting with her brother at a local grocery store. She timed it and had a accountability person come and get her at the end of 15 minutes, to ensure that the meeting was short. She and her brother walked around the store and talked a little. During that meeting, completely unknown to the Christian presentation despite prayer, her brother gave a message to her cult parts. Due to the message, for months her cult parts strongly attempted to sabotage some very important matters for the person. These parts shared what happened only six months later in therapy, after much trouble.

Asking the Christian presenters/Host if the survivor was safe during a time period may not work for several reasons:

- The false Christian Host was the one actually out praying and reporting how the trip went, and the survivor is completely unaware of this fact

- The Christian presentation/Host has been heavily programmed to sabotage healing and keep cult contact up. They will be completely unaware of this fact. The person's day to day Christian presentation/Host may be the most heavily programmed part of the person, and they will not know this at all. The cult will not leave Christian parts unprogrammed; and in fact, will make sure these are the ones that maintain recontact.

How Do You Prevent Re-accessing?

Now that the problem of accessing has been defined, what can the survivor, and their helper do, to prevent reaccessing? Especially with the knowledge that early in therapy, reaccessing occurs in nearly 100 % of survivors? It is very common for survivors to be given cover memories that they "broke free" or that the cult abuse ended earlier in life, while in reality, they have been continuously cult active. It is common for survivors to be reaccessed or have cult contact of some kind, until the amnesia starts coming down.

The cult does not just "let people go" when they become adults, or enter therapy. Instead, **the accessing will often increase during this time**, as cults or government agencies do not want to lose members.

With this knowledge, the survivor will need to find out which parts are currently in contact with the cult. One way to do so is to give up all phone, email and online activity for a period of time, such as two months. The parts who are currently contacting will probably complain loudly, or the survivor may even become suicidal. The person may become restless and feel a huge urgency that they are "missing something important" in emails or online (the survivor will always have legitimate sounding reasons for continuing online and phone activities, such as checking bank statements and paying bills, but behind these is their programming to recontact running). The Christian presentation, with support, then has the opportunity to bring truth to these parts and help them break out of their cult-trained beliefs.

The desire to stop cult contact must come from the survivor themselves. While it may be obvious to the therapist and others that the survivor is being re-accessed, they will be oblivious to this fact, and will become very angry/defensive/hostile if confronted about this.

It can be helpful to educate the survivor and their parts on why it is a good idea to stop cult (family) contact. Some reasons to do so include:

- The survivor gets hurt

- Loved ones of the survivor get hurt when they are accessed
- Accessing impedes healing, because parts get retraumatized
- It is an extremely poor Christian witness to people who are still in the cult
- It is an extremely poor Christian witness to the survivor's own parts
- It is a lifestyle of extreme duplicity
- The survivor has to actually hurt others during a reaccessing session
- The survivor may be forced to accept agendas against their therapist and other survivors
- Cult loyal parts that recontact will be rewarded for contact, which actually increases the bonding to those reaccessing, making healing more difficult

There are always significant traumas and double binds behind recontact programming, and the therapist will want to help the survivor look at these issues. Cult loyal parts will have difficulty stopping recontact if they believe that failure to do so results in the torture or death of someone they love. This is where the ability to trust the LORD with the safety of double binds is so important.

Saying, "LORD, I give my double binds to you," does not at all ensure that this is being done. Instead, HOW the double binds were installed, and with whom, and the specific vows to protect the double bind will need to be remembered. Often, these vows are elicited by the survivor watching a double bind being tortured; unable to take any more, the survivor will cave and agree to stay in contact. They will have no memory of this event, since they will also agree to forget the event, or else their loved one will be tortured. This is why consistent memory work and dedication to healing and looking at the events that run recontact programming inside are so important.

If the survivor is an international survivor (one who was hosted in several countries as a child and adult) their primary double binds will likely be in another country, and they may be amnesic to them. This will also need to be looked at. Breaking double binds with the American family may not be sufficient to stop re-accessing if there are unconscious double binds elsewhere.

The survivor's first programmer/trainer will often be their primary double bind.

They will often be completely amnesic to whom this person actually is. Their systems will be invested in protecting this person above all others, and so they will disclose other people as double binds first. The true double binds often will not come out until later in therapy.

This is where accountability can help. Until the survivor is aware of and has broken their recontact programming, and has truly dealt with their double binds, outside accountability can help prevent reaccess.

Safe accountability would be either a **non-dissociative person** or a survivor who has broken their own double binds and recontact programming and is co-conscious with their most loyal cult parts.

Survivors who are in the early stages of healing should <u>never</u> be asked to be accountability for another survivor's safety. They will be completely unaware of the fact that they themselves have a strong recontact agenda, which can include helping other survivors "reconnect" with family (cult) members, or others.

A safe accountability person should be made aware of the survivor's safety plan (any survivor should have a safety plan, if they are serious about stopping re-accessing). This will include awareness of any phone calls and texts made and received, and any online activities of any kind; for instance, the survivor may ask the accountability person to be with them and watching at all times that they go online.

Failure to have accountability jeopardizes both the survivor and others that they could impact. While it can be a "bother" to have accountability, the alternative can be much more painful.

Once the survivor stops Internet, phone and other contact, and has accountability in place, they may actually feel worse for a period of time as they are breaking the programming. The programming is actually being drawn out so the survivor can look at it: they may feel suicidal or depressed, or shaky for a period of time. This will pass as the programming is broken.

Stopping Astral Access

If the cult cannot reach the survivor by physical means, they will attempt to do so spiritually, often through astral projection. These demonic spirits will appear, often in the middle of the night, to the survivor, and will frequently appear as double binds/loved ones. The astrals may appear to be in great distress, and will attempt to "blackmail" the survivor into recontact with messages that the loved one is being tortured, or sobbing that they miss the survivor.

The survivor will need to discover and close the spiritual doors that allow spiritual access. This process will include:

- Finding out which parts inside have the job to maintain spiritual contact with loved ones in the group.
- Why they want to continue this contact
- What these parts believe will happen if contact is stopped.

It is common to feel immense fear at first, at the thought of stopping astral contact, since the rituals and programming done around this is extensive, and starts in infancy. Spiritual parts may attempt to punish the survivor for attempting to stop it, until they become aware of the danger of continuing it.

Once all doors are closed, both spiritually and physically, parts may start feeling safe enough to come out and disclose to the survivor, and heal. This includes getting rid of the demonic spirits that sit within the parts whose job is to maintain astral contact, and resolving the traumas that they have undergone.

Over time, astral contact will lessen as the survivor learns to use their authority to stop the contact. Simply commanding an astral to depart in the name of the true Jesus is sufficient to make it leave; doing this builds faith in the survivor's parts and witnesses to them over time, and they will be more and more willing to turn to the Christian God instead of to the demonic.

Chapter 4: Dealing with Emotions

One of the most difficult issues for survivors who are trying to heal from cult-related mind control to deal with is emotions. Why is this?

In cases of extensive programming, the individual will have been tortured since they were in the womb, with one primary goal in mind: control of the person. As part of the dissociation, the individual will be taught to "give away" their emotions to demons and parts, whom they are told can "relieve" them of this intense pain.

Many times, controller parts (parts who are in charge over other parts or internal systems) will be highly logical, or be programmed to believe that they are "ascended" (above "mortal" feelings, which are considered base, earth-bound, and physical). The higher-order, or ascended systems in a survivor's psyche will have been taught, and believe since earliest infancy (or before) false beliefs such as:

- They are gods, angels or demons
- They are ascended beings
- They are immortals
- They have overcome their humanity
- They do not feel pain
- **They do not have human emotions**

This belief is based upon immense emotional and physical trauma. The types of traumas that create this type of belief can include:

- Killing the birth mother when the infant is born – and telling the infant it is his/her fault (this is very common in organized occultic groups, and creates great internal guilt which is used to control the individual, who is told they are a "mother killer" and other equally painful lies)
- Torturing the fetus in the womb, and telling them that the pain they feel is the "pain of mortality" and the only way to escape the pain is to "ascend" (by taking on a demonic or spiritual identity and spirit, which then shields from the emotional and physical pain, but continues the delusion and deception that the individual is an "ascended being" instead

of a human being who has been heavily traumatized

The "Difficult Emotions" for survivors

Most presenter parts (the ones who normally enter into therapy) in survivors of mind control will have great difficulty in identifying or expressing their emotions in a healthy way. This is the result of a combination of factors which can include:

- Dissociation of strong feelings (programming to not feel; with a very stoic or numb presentation)

- Role models (parents, trainers, others) who were very unhealthy or abusive in their expression of emotions, and dismissed any expressions of feelings by the survivor throughout childhood (except to punish them)

- Unconscious fear that the emotion will overwhelm the survivor and they will not be able to handle it

Some emotions are particularly difficult for survivors to identify or express in healthy ways. But with healing, emotions do come, often with "flooding" when they first occur, until the traumatic events are dealt with, and the parts that underwent trauma can be comforted.

Anger/rage

This emotion can be difficult for a survivor to deal with, because rage was often "sent" to parts whose job was to torture, punish or kill either external people or internal parts. As a child, while undergoing close quarters combat training, or during martial arts training, they are told to "tap into" the rage to help increase their endurance and ability. Unconsciously, the survivor may associate anger/rage with these activities, and avoid their expression completely in their presentation. Alternatively, the survivor may have a very aggressive/hostile presentation that feels protected from sorrow, loneliness or rejection through responding with anger in situations that trigger these feelings. Either way, many survivors have difficulty processing and expressing intense anger or rage in an appropriate way.

They may fear that they will "lose control" or even "kill someone" if the rage they fear comes forward.

It is important to help the survivor find ways to express the rage that has built up over the years, and develop connections between unfeeling parts and those that feel. This is done over time, with the "non-feelers" gradually developing the capacity to feel, and to comfort the parts that may feel overwhelmed with feelings.

Anger, or any other emotion, often comes in strongly, peaks within two to three days, then gradually begins to subside (the amount of time in the cycle will vary with the survivor, the amount of trauma, and the amount of support available to them). It can help to reassure the survivor that these feelings will NOT last forever, even though tapping into a lifetime of dissociated feeling can seem that way at first.

It can help to develop methods of coping with rage when it occurs. The activities that help most will differ with each person; for some, vigorous physical activity (hiking, running, boxing) or hitting a box with a bat will help. Hitting rocks with a sledge hammer (with goggles and protection worn) can also help. Using a therapy bat, and hitting a bed or other safe object can also help. Others break ice as anger relief. It is important to have some accountability/supervision when first doing anger work because of the amount of emotion (which may seem scary to the survivor) coming out; and the possible need to be "talked down."

In some instances, when a survivor gets in touch with the abuse memories and the associated rage, they may become homicidal for a short period of time. Often, they may verbalize wanting to go find the perpetrator, and do to them what was done to the survivor. It is important to assess the degree of actual risk, and create a safety plan. The survivor needs to realize that going back and hurting perpetrators will place them in extreme jeopardy: they will be immediately accessed and tortured themselves in most cases; or, they will be harmed spiritually should they succeed in hurting the perpetrator.

Forgiveness is an important component of healing, but it cannot be rushed. All too often in Christian circles, there is a rush to put the Band-Aid of the words "I forgive them" without fully processing the extent of the loss the survivor incurred. This includes the rage at God that a survivor feels, because ultimately, they blame Him for what they have been through. This will be addressed further in the chapter on anti-Christian programming.

Guilt

Guilt is an extremely painful emotion for most survivors, for several reasons.

1. It is often installed during prenatal programming, during which the fetus is asked if they want to live, or for the other (implanted zygotes) to live. During the first months of life after conception, the fetus will always respond "yes" – and then the zygote the programmer wished to get rid of is killed. This happens over the succeeding weeks until there is only one embryo left – an embryo that experiences a lot of survivor guilt due to the death of the other embryos in the womb. This prenatal guilt programming was first developed by Mengele, and is one of the foundations on which self-punishment, penance, punisher and other programming is placed.
2. Throughout infancy and childhood, the survivor will have been taught to punish

themselves. In a typical setup, if the survivor disobeys or hesitates, they are punished brutally for failure; or, someone they love (a twin, brother or sister, or beloved trainer) is punished for their failure. This causes extreme distress, and the child promises never to fail again. Internalized images of these loved ones are then punished if the child disobeys.

3. The survivor will have blood guilt through participation in rites, rituals and sacrifices throughout a lifetime. If they are a trained assassin, this guilt increases, and the survivor may find it difficult to believe that God could truly forgive them.

4. The survivor, as they recover memories, will eventually remember being a perpetrator, being forced to torture other infants, children, birth mothers, or to participate in other acts such as rape or punishing others. Most organized cult members are able to do at least basic programming on others, since this is a skill taught from earliest childhood in most groups. The survivor will then recover memories of becoming what they hated most – an abuser – and will need to deal with the resulting guilt.

5. If the survivor has anti-Christian programming (and most do), they will have been forced to hurt an actor portraying "Jesus" or to nail other children to crosses, and to do acts that show their hatred of God and Christianity. They are then told, "God can never forgive you, He hates you because you did this" and the child believes this.

The survivor will need to hear frequently that God loves them and forgives them, since they will question this many times. They may have great difficulty believing that someone who has committed the deeds they have committed can ever be forgiven.

Scriptures about the love of God can be helpful (although be aware that these may also have been used in anti-Christian programming), as well as books about forgiveness and grace; being kind to the survivor, and showing/modeling love and acceptance are helpful during this time of emotional struggle. The survivor and their parts will need to come to a point of finally accepting that what God says in His word is true: they are forgiven, regardless of what they have done, in spite of how they feel.

Shame

Shame is another painful emotion that many survivors experience. The survivor may feel shame regarding their sexual abuse, and the terrible forms this can take in occultic and mind control settings (including bestiality, necrophilia, prostitution, child abuse, infant abuse, etc.). They may feel shame because they were unable to fight the programmers; or because they "caved" or gave in to programming, or did things they hated doing.

Shame is the survivor labeling themselves negatively because of what they have done, and what they believe others think about them. Healing takes time, with lots of acceptance, the opportunity to process memories, and the abuse and degradation stopping. Again, providing love and helping the survivor understand they are accepted by others and by God, and that what they did was not their fault, can help. Often, they "caved" under conditions that would be intolerable for anyone; support people showing that the survivor is not judged by them is important to healing.

Rejection

Many survivors experience rejection at numerous levels. They may experience:

- Self-rejection due to terrible wounds in the womb, such as the birth mother being injected with drugs that cause tremendous uterine pain; she will then scream to "get it out!" or something similar, causing a deep rejection wound in the fetus.
- Childhood rejections as part of the abandonment programming designed to bond the child only to those the group wants them to bond to. It is quite common for the parents in host families to reject or ridicule the child, to prevent their bonding with them, which would interfere with the child bonding with the trainers.
- Rejection by members of the group if they try to leave; if the survivor is reaccessed, they will be kicked around, tortured, raped, and told that they are "evil", a "traitor" and other things; members of the group will urinate and defecate on the survivor to show how they feel about them.
- Rejection by Christians who do not understand cult or mind control abuse, find it "scary" and who ask the survivor to leave their church; or who silently shun the survivor.

Rejection is painful, and is a base of recontact programming (i.e. "nobody can love you but the group"). The survivor will need support as they deal with their rejection and abandonment memories, and attempt to work at detaching from the cult, and attaching with non-cult support (which can seem frightening, since they may have no idea of how to do this). Understanding, empathy and caring can help the survivor through this painful time of experiencing the pain beneath their programming. By modeling acceptance, supporters are teaching the survivor how to accept themselves; the love of God is also critical to healing rejection wounds.

Loneliness

Most survivors battle loneliness through much of their journey. They are leaving a group that contains their deepest, most intimate relationships, and attempting to heal in a world that often does not understand what the survivor is going through (unless they are fortunate enough to find a good, knowledgeable therapist or support person).

The deepest loneliness a survivor may face is for themselves. The cult has taken away their history; caused them to dissociate their deepest feelings, and this causes a deep ache for truth and connection with the "real me" inside. Basically, the survivor is lonely for their core, who holds some of the strongest feelings and beliefs inside, and who has been carefully hidden beneath numerous layers of programming and demonic.

Again, a supportive, nonjudgmental relationship is important as the survivor works through the issues surrounding developing healthy, safe support. A real danger when loneliness hits is that the survivor, who misses loved ones in the cult, will rush to make new friends without prayer or discernment first. It is very common for cult groups to "send" friends or romantic relationships to survivors who are attempting to leave the group. They will seem well-meaning, caring, and very supportive of the survivor's healing; but they will often have a job to do in their back parts.

It is also common for survivors to seek friendship with other survivors, but if the other survivors are unhealed (i.e. early in their healing journey and unaware of current cult activity), it is quite common for them to access one another, and pull each other back into cult activity. The survivor should always proceed with caution, and pray for discernment, before befriending another survivor; since they themselves could also be used in this way without conscious knowledge.

Sorrow/grieving

When a survivor breaks free of a cult group, they will go through a period of grieving. This is normal; although the abuse has stopped, they often will not feel "happy" for a long time. This is because they have cut off every meaningful relationship in their life, other than with God, and must take the time to grieve this loss. Yes, the relationships were abusive; yes, these people hurt the survivor. But these people are the survivor's mother, father, brother, sister, children, best friends, and giving up their entire support system is extremely difficult.

The survivor who gets out of a cult knows better than most what Jesus meant by "counting the cost" to become free. They will also face grieving because of threats against the loved ones who did not get out; for many survivors, these threats are communicated through hand signals as people pass by them in a mall; through subliminals online or on their cell phone; through videos of a loved one being tortured sent to their email address, or even direct contact (such as a loved one showing up weeping, who raises their shirt to show the bruises and cuts on their back that they endured because the survivor left).

When the survivor is grieving, it is important to sit with them, figuratively speaking, and let them mourn. They may be numb, in emotional shock, or they may cry nonstop for days at a time. They will want to talk about the loved ones left behind, and need to do this, to process the ending of the relationship as they knew it.

It does not help to continuously point out to the survivor that these people were evil abusers. They know this, deep inside; but they also love these people. This love/hate is what bonded them to the cult and to doing their jobs; and is part of why they dissociated. Bringing down dissociation will involve remembering and grieving for these loved ones left behind. Processing the grief will vary with the individual. Writing a letter to the loved one(s)(that is never mailed); planting a "memorial bush", creating a collage, are all ways some have worked on their grief.

With time, grief does heal, and the survivor will be able to work on developing new relationships. It is important that the survivor allows themselves this time.

Hopeless Despair

Hopeless despair is one of the most painful feelings that survivors can experience. It can be caused by:

- Extreme loss, including seeing loved ones tortured to death because the survivor is trying to leave the group; the programmers then blame the survivor for the death(s)
- Programmed despair (programming to believe that the survivor can never heal; or that God can never forgive them)
- Technology torture: this involves the brain being hit by microbursts of high frequency or low frequency waves in various locations, to stimulate the brain to experience extreme despair
- Core attachment pain coming forward: the realization that the survivor has been abused, manipulated, tortured and betrayed since conception by the people they bonded to most deeply; this creates the despair that it was "all for nothing" that the survivor performed for the group and survived torture over a lifetime (for the love of people that they now realize horrifically abused them)

When the survivor is in hopeless despair, it does **not** help to:

- quote scriptures at them (although this will help at a future time),
- Tell them to "get their act together" or ask them "where is your faith?" since they already feel bad enough

What does help is to acknowledge to them that you understand that they are in deep pain, and sit with them and synchronize. This is one of the most difficult things a support person can do, since you will want to "rescue" the person from their pain, or feel bad that you can't help them feel better right away. The LORD is the one who will minister to the survivor, as they get in touch with their feelings and they express the feelings to Him.

You can encourage the individual to write a letter to God, expressing to Him how they feel; to pray directly, sharing their despair with Him, and to spend time then asking Him to minister to their pain. The Holy Spirit is able to bring comfort and hope to the hopeless, regardless of the situation that has caused the despair, since Jesus experienced to the full everything – the agony of sin, loss and emotional pain – on the cross to redeem and heal these wounds.

Core attachment pain takes time to work through, and cannot be rushed (please see chapter on "Working with the Core" for more on this topic).

Sexual Feelings

Most survivors will have a lifetime of sexual abuse and programming in their history. Many groups train their toddlers and preschoolers to act as "black widows" who seduce and then kill individuals; or who infiltrate sex parties of the wealthy (where pedophilia is often rampant) to gather information about the participants.

Sexual programming is installed from earliest infancy in most survivors. Programmers will sexually abuse the infants during diaper changes; during bonding times, and will sexually torture the infants while tech stimulating the pleasure centers in the brain to create sadomasochistic parts that enjoy sexual torture.

The infants are stretched with special instruments so by the time they are two, they can accommodate an adult penis without damage. Infants are stimulated to experience multiple orgasms with vibrators as a "reward" for performance.

Everyone the survivor knows and loves has sexually abused them, and this is considered part of a "love" bond, which creates soul and demonic ties. The survivor may never have experienced any relationship in their life that did not involve sexual abuse, and they may have sexual parts come out that "test" the supporter.

Simply put, the survivor has been raised in a highly sexualized environment, and at first, will not understand or know what to do with the feelings that come up. If they are in a truly safe house, the time spent there may be the first days since birth that the survivor has not had sex with someone. In 7 X 7 programming, one of the torture lines will be extreme sexual arousal, designed to cause the survivor to seek out a sexual partner (with resulting reaccessing); or to turn to demonic sex for relief.

Information may have been downloaded to the individual while they were in a sexually aroused state, which is a natural amnesia barrier, since the information can normally only be recovered when the individual is in that state (although with the LORD's help, the information can be recovered without arousal).

How can the survivor cope with feelings that can produce shame in the presentation, possible annoyance in the helper if they attempt seduction, or painful body sensations?
First, it can help to acknowledge that the feelings are there. It is not the survivor's fault that this was installed, and they need to realize that this too can be forgiven.

The survivor will need support as they grieve the sheer extent of the abuse; and with breaking soul ties with former sexual partners. Deliverance from lust and other demonic can help decrease the severity.

If the survivor chooses chastity (recommended for spiritual and safety reasons) they will need to be in prayer over these feelings; they do decrease over time as the survivor chooses to not act out on the feelings. Acceptance of the parts, and helping them to see that it is possible to be loved without automatic sexual abuse is a big component of healing, since it brings new information to these parts, and a new worldview to operate from.

At times, these parts will feel hurt or offended if the support person does not take them up on their offers; after all, this is how people "love" one another in their worldview. With time, patience and caring, they will come to understand that someone can truly care for them without wanting a sexual relationship.

Terror

When a survivor begins to work hard at undoing their programming, often there will be retaliation from internal punishment and reprogramming systems – and they will feel terror. This terror is instilled purposely, from the first tortures in the womb (such as when the trainers cut off fetal digits, which regrow if done early in development) to the most recent access.
The terror is often based upon highly realistic virtual reality, which replays the infant's prime terrors. These include:

- Being dropped rapidly (startle reflex)
- Being skinned alive
- Being burned
- Being drowned/suffocated/buried alive
- Rats chewing on the infant
- Bugs stinging the infant
- Prime bonds (people loved most) are shown falling apart and in agony, or with blood spurting out of their bodies

There are others. Entire terror lines are installed, with the purpose of controlling the survivor. These terrors are often encapsulated in the framework of a "hell" created by the programmers, with different levels playing out different terror scenarios (such as the internal parts being tied to a stake inside "hell level 2" and "demons" which originally were cult actors in infancy, and later are internal parts that took on this identity torturing the survivor by burning them alive).

At base level, fetal and infantile terror drive many punishment and recontact programs. This can be experienced as restless, the feeling that "something is wrong" and if the survivor continues to not recontact, can escalate to panic, then terror. Night terrors are common, since the survivor will be programmed with dreams of punishment and terror if they stop contact, or astrals may come to remind the survivor of the terrible fate awaiting them if they fail to recontact. Core terror (the belief that the universe will fall apart and turn black, and all people the survivor loves will die, and they themselves will be "unmade" if they continue healing) makes it difficult for the survivor to face dismantling deep programmed beliefs and systems internally. The terror was installed for this very purpose.

The survivor will often feel as if they are "losing it", "going psychotic" or "losing their mind, and can't stand a single second more of this" as the dissociated emotions come forward. This is based upon programmed beliefs that if the survivor tries to dismantle their own programming, they will go insane; they may be given drugs, tech torture and setups to "prove" this belief.

They really are not losing their mind, but they will feel this way as the terror hits. It can help to ground the survivor to here and now (feeling the ground beneath their feet, touching something soft, or warm, or cool; hearing music) when terror hits. Getting rid of the demonic that holds the programming in place (by repenting of the rituals and sacrifices performed before and after installation by the survivor to seal it in, and repenting of the agreement for installation) can also help.

Remind the survivor that they survived the event happening the first time, and they can survive remembering. Remind them that if they attempted to "break programming" in the lab (as programmers will tell them to do, in setups designed to make the survivor believe they cannot break programming without trauma), that it was a **setup;** that now, they have safety, prayer and support that they did not have during the setups.

Terror does decrease over time. The survivor will likely abreact some of the more terror-producing traumas, as internal parts come forward, seeking healing and relief from the awful reality that they experience inside. With support, prayer, and time, the LORD does heal these parts, and the survivor will experience fewer and weaker bouts of panic as they continue to heal.

Chapter 5: Presentation Programming

It is a common misconception that "hosts" or "presenters" have been protected, or have undergone less programming or trauma than other systems. On the contrary, the presentation is often one of the most extensively programmed systems in the survivor of international occultic programming. It can be some of the most difficult programming to dismantle since basically, this involves looking at their own programming.

In most international occultic groups, the child spends the first three years fulltime at a cult facility, being continuously programmed. At age three, the child will also be placed within several host families around the world. The child may grow up with anywhere from four to seven families in different countries, and will spend several weeks, or even a month or two each year, with each family during the next 20 years. School photos are taken, and a cover identity created in the countries which they anticipate the child will be working for them as they grow older into adulthood. The families will be given photos of the child (or a look-alike) in infancy for photo albums.

These host families will have programming to prevent the child and the host parents from bonding with each other, since **the child must always maintain their primary bond with the primary programmers. The true host and core will always only be allowed to bond with these programmers.**

An example of host families could be one in Germany, one in France, one in Amsterdam, one in the United States, and even one in Israel. Since many occultic groups hate Israel, and a focus of their intelligence efforts is infiltration of Israeli national security, they will attempt as often as possible to place a child within Israel with a trainer who acts as their "aunt" or "uncle." The child rotates between these host families and **thus learns to rotate between presentations based upon their current living situation**. The child has already learned to never speak any language but that of the host family (on pain of severe punishment), and has already undergone numerous experiences prior to going to a host family to teach them to not bond with anyone except the programmers.

Detachment Training

For example, at age two, the child will be allowed to interact with and bond with a loving woman, who acts as a mother surrogate to the child who is hungry for nurturing by a woman. After several weeks of loving interactions, at some point, the woman will turn around and begin severely abusing the child, such as by pushing them down stairs, sexually abusing them, or other abuse, laughing at the child's display of pain at the emotional betrayal. The child must learn the lesson to never trust anyone, or to bond with anyone other than the primary trainers, or they will be killed.

The host families will also be programmed to reject the child, and/or abuse the child, to ensure that the child does not create a bond that is too strong. **The primary bond will always be an unconscious one, that the Christian and cult cover presentations are completely amnesic to**: a primary trainer whom they love greatly, since this is the only person they were allowed to love during their early childhood.

MI6 Training

Once the host presentations are in place, the child (by age 3 ½) will undergo training at MI6. MI6 has a special area (known as "Colonel Green's House" after Colonel Green, the founder of MI6) where young children undergo specialized assassin and military training. Again, the child goes there with their class, and is assigned a number. Instead of being called by name, they will be called "42" or a similar number during training and learn to respond to this.

MI6 reserves the Green House for certain groups at specific times, and the trainers during this time are all programmers for the group that work for MI6. The child will perfect previous skills taught to them as a toddler in using a gun; their delta computer system will be built to greater complexity, and their ability to classify intelligence, and store it based upon its classification will be perfected during this time. The ability to use a photographic visual and auditory memory, and download to handlers information obtained while on a mission, is also perfected.

They will perfect basic skills of all operatives, such as following a target, dropping a tail, and blending in inconspicuously in a group.

The terrible punishments used at MI6 (such as the room with walls that move inwards, or the multi-faceted crystal ball in a room with mirrors used when the child is drugged, or the specialized computer system that is used for delta installation) are all used on the child. By the time the child has completed the 3-month training course (which is updated as they grow older), they will have a firm base in military special operations. By age 12, the child will have developed enough skillsets that they will be classified as a military weapon.

Delta Computer Training

Delta training is extensive enough to give it special mention. During delta training, the child will be hooked up to a computer, which it will be taught to emulate while in delta state. The computer speaks with a synthetic, very robotic voice, and the child will do the same. The delta training will encompass high and low delta states, and the child will be taught to classify all cognitive thoughts and experiences according to security levels. Low security levels can be retained as conscious thought; any information classified as mid to high security will be "access denied" to conscious presentation thought, and stored within the deeper delta states of the brain.

The delta computer system will have a ground zero state, with delta controllers and introjected trainers "manning" the computer systems. At ground zero, primary traumas and death state programming are installed, to prevent dismantling of the computer system and to keep the child invested in protecting high-security information.

Psyche, along with Mnemosyne (amnesia) will have the jobs of maintaining the separation between conscious (known) and unknown information. Psyche never forgets, and Mnemosyne never remembers, and both control the flow of information within delta.

Theta Controller Training

As the child reaches late preschool and early school age, they will undergo Galileo training (training in remote viewing, mind reading and thought influencing), in order to provide their handlers with access to buildings and conversations they would otherwise be unable to reach. During a mission, a child will be asked, for example, to go into an office building, and "read" classified or private documents during the night hours and then share what they have read with their handlers.

The child will also have the ability to introject themselves and images or thoughts into other people's dream states. In fact, part of theta assassin training is learning to have the subject dream of their own death. The head theta controller (such as Nemesis) will oversee the others, including Phobos (fear); Thantos (death) and Chaos (insanity). Theta training is aimed at teaching the child to induce each of these states in others using demonic powers developed.

Theta Assassin Training

The higher occultic groups at times attempt to induce death in those that cross them. If a child is sent on a mission, they will have sexual relations with the "mark." At a later time (often days later), the child will be sent back spiritually with a mentor back to the mark, to cause their death while sleeping. This will often begin with a terrifying dream of the individual's death, and many have literally died of fright due to these terrible dreams.

Some of the leaders of top occultic organizations will have theta guards composed of individuals who have completed their theta training (these guards can range in age from 12 years old to 32). The guards sit in front of an office, for example, as a warning to any intruders.

The newer generations of thetas have highly developed "kill" training in the spiritual realm developed from the first weeks of life in the womb on, and are often mentored by groups of very skilled theta trainers to prevent the children from turning on the trainers and killing them. These newer super thetas have poorly developed presentations, and must often live very protected lives away from the public eye.

Secrecy/Amnesia Training

Some of the most important training the preschooler undergoes is secrecy training. The child has bonded heavily to and wants to protect the primary trainers, and so they are told: "If you betray us, we could be killed. The only way to not betray us is to not remember." The child **willingly** agrees to amnesia, in order to protect the people they love most.

In other secrecy setups, a child will complete a setup "mission" and later is asked if they remembered what happened. If the child answers "Yes" a gun is placed to their head, and they are told that if they remember, the programmer must kill them. They are asked again if they remember (presenters are asked); until the child is either completely amnesic, or is killed (the occultic groups do not allow children who have any memory traces to live; the gun threat is very real).

Another setup is "remember the flowers": the child is taken to a garden at a place where he/she has spent times chatting with their favorite programmer in the past. There is a water pool in the middle of the garden, and during this setup, it is filled with corpses of children the same age as the young child (ages 2 or 3). The programmer cuts a flower, gives it to the child and tells the child to "remember the flowers" (i.e. the dead children who remembered and told others).

There are many, many examples of such secrecy setups, from being buried alive for a day, and the child being told that they will be buried forever if they ever tell (the child is also forced to watch the burial of a child who "told" and several days later help exhume the corpse, as a visual reminder of what can happen); to being buried in a casket filled with bugs, a rotten corpse, or other objects.

The child may be placed in a box with bees that sting them (after going through several weeks of anti-venom therapy previously) as a reminder that "memories hurt."

They are also forced to view the deaths of "traitors" who betrayed the programmers, including crucifixions (the class is marched every three hours past the three crosses for three days to watch the effect on the dying men); and the torture of others who remembered and "told."

Alice in Wonderland Programming

Most members of occultic international groups will have at least one presentation that goes by the name "Alice" for a reason: this is a trigger for Wonderland programming. By age five, the child will be taken to a large estate in France (or, other locations, depending on the group) for Alice in Wonderland programming. This is an elaborate setup, and occurs over the period of a week. The child enters through rooms that reinforce previous training ("control the children": is recorded and replayed, with pictures of dead children displayed on the walls of the room; mirrors, "remember the flowers" and other triggers). They then enter a "backward world" where everything is backwards (much like the third dimension; this prepares the child for this travel). **Alice (representing the presentation main controller who is heavily demonized)** guides the child through backwards houses, where people walk and talk backwards (a common cause of childhood dyslexia is the confusion this creates).

The child is then taken to a setup street where things are not backwards, but "crooked" or off slightly, which is even more disorienting. The child must walk with Alice and the Cheshire Cat leading them through houses where things are insanely wrong, where people talk nonsense, and the floors and roofs may be upside down, to teach the child not to trust reality.

Alice then brings the child at last to a place where they see the white rabbit (who represents the primary trainer), and they follow him "down the hole" (representing amnesia) to a room where the presentation stays behind, watching a movie **(screen memories**); the back parts then take the child's body through the rest of the setup. They enter a garden with animated/demonic flowers that at first talk kindly to the child, but later turn on the child and attack them. Wasps come and sting the child, and the large caterpillar (the guardian of the garden, played by another primary bond) tells the child what to do, and how to escape.

The child then enters a huge maze created from hedges. Soon, they are pursued by the "Jabberwocky" (a demonic presence and strong presentation punisher), and must rely upon their theta skills to run and escape, and even leave the body and fly away. The white rabbit and the Cheshire Cat lead the child to safety, but at times will try to "trick" the child **until the child learns to rely on themselves** instead of these capricious demonic "helpers."

The child sleeps outdoors, trying to get out of the hedge, and runs across the queen of hearts (a primary double bind, often a twin sister) and her court playing croquet (with the severed heads of human children used as the balls). The queen becomes very interested in using the child's head (the child is constantly called "Alice" throughout the setup, to represent the presentations, since Alice in Wonderland is ultimately presentation programming to remain amnesic and rely on demonic help to do so).

The demonic "Alice" and Cheshire cat help "rescue" the child, who then goes through the "valley of the shadow of death." In the middle is a cottage; it is now nighttime, and the weary child knocks at the door, to be greeted by a kindly woman. The child is fed, sleeps, and is warned to avoid the Jabberwocky, which seeks to kill the child. Once the programming is installed, the Jabberwocky acts as a presentation punisher, punishing the presenters for remembering or disobeying cult directives.

During the night, the kindly woman gets up. The child is awake, vomiting from the effects of a mild poison they were given in the food. The woman calls in her familiars (wolves) and tries to kill the child, who cries out for help to "Alice" and the "Cheshire Cat" to rescue her. A mage also comes and helps rescue the child, who continues the journey, meeting other characters. Finally, the child ends up at the palace of the Queen of Hearts, who demands a sacrifice (the child was already told that the last child to complete the Alice scenarios will be her sacrifice). The children who live watch the final child come in and be sacrificed in a ritual. This reminds them to never be slow or tardy when coming to a "party" (ritual). The "parties" in the Alice in Wonderland books are always referring to rituals.

Alice will go to a tea party, where her "mother" (Nemosyn, a strong amnesia controller) shows up. As the party progresses, one by one, the people at the party are killed in horrendously gruesome ways. The horrified Alice is reminded by Nemosyn that "everything is fine" and is told to "let me take care of everything." If Alice agrees, Nemosyn then "takes away" the memories of the murders and sacrifices, and the characters are removed one by one. Finally, there are no bodies left, and Nemosyn assures Alice that "nothing bad ever happened."

Crazy Alice Programming

A subset of the Alice in Wonderland (presenter) programming is the "Crazy Alice" programming, which is meant to warn the Alice controller over the presentation to never allow memories to come up, or they will be labeled "insane" and extreme abuse will occur. This is often the root of insanity fears when a person first starts remembering their past.

In this setup (also in France for some groups), the child (now called "Alice") is taken to a mental institution where the inmates are chained, and who rant, rave and curse at her. She is left there for days, with her only food being rancid water and rotten cabbage. The inmates hurl feces at her, verbally abuse her, and the custodians sexually abuse her while she is chained to the wall because of her "insanity" (remembering).

Because she is "sick", and "mentally ill" Alice is taken regularly down to the basement for "treatment" which consists of electroshocks, drowning, and being held over a rat pit filled with hungry rats that are allowed to bite her feet and ankles. The child is told repeatedly that "remembering" or "telling" will have her labeled "crazy" and that she will be taken to the institution (or one similar) for "treatment." This is part of developing the presenter amnesia and vows to never remember (or seek treatment). During the hospital stay, a team of doctors in white coats walk through the ward and stay with Alice, saying, "Here's our favorite patient" (the main doctor is the child's primary programmer). Alice will keep a stuffed rabbit with her ("foo foo") who at night seems to come alive and sexually abuses her (this is done with a hand puppet). When Alice reports the abuse the next day, the doctors look at her sadly, and insist that she is "sick" and "needs more treatment."

There is a special room in the "hospital" for the religiously insane, with Bible studies and church meetings, where Alice is raped and abused by the "Christians" in the hospital.

Black Alice Programming

In another version of Alice programming, Alice has a "dark side" that comes out and kills everyone around her in a killing spree. The terrified presenter wakes up to a room full of bloody bodies, and is told that if she ever remembers, the "evil" inside of her will "escape" and she will kill her loved ones. This is a particularly cruel form of amnesia programming.

Wizard of Oz Programming

This programming is also often done first during the preschool years, when the child can most easily internalize the program. The dark core ("Dorothy") is taken to another dimension, with her goal always to return to the Emerald City (representing ascension and the celestial paradise). The programming represents travel through the dimensions, the dangers involved, and the rewards for "ascending."

The goal of Wizard of Oz programming is to remind the child that they must always contact, or return home; and to create great fear of remembering (or, they will be placed in a coma and never wake up, unlike Dorothy in Oz, who woke up from "death" only after returning home." It also represents the need to "never leave the path" (presenter programming to stay on the path given to them, or disaster results).

Fantasia Programming

Walt Disney was an avowed Illuminist, and his goal when creating Disney productions was to introduce the general public to the occult, especially young children, and to reinforce programming in those raised in the occult.

For instance, animals often "talk" in Disney films, and people can turn into animals, which are actually mage spells. The images are often dark and demonic in the animated movies, and have become increasingly so in recent years.

Disney's favorite film was Fantasia, in which he took classical music that was used to program young children with, and developed highly occultic themes in the cartoons that accompany it. To the untrained eye, Fantasia seems a bit odd; but the individual in the occult understands that the themes of a mage in training ("the sorcerer's assistant) who must turn to his more powerful mentor for help, and the Greek pantheon (in the famous rain sequence), mythology and even the depiction of an occultic ritual and then the famous strains of *ave maria* (a common programming tune) end the film.

Fantasia is blatant occultic imagery throughout, and was used extensively in the 1950s through 1970s to program individuals with. It was superseded in recent years by movies such as the Matrix, which depicts high-level programming, Labyrinth, and more recently, Frozen.

Helping the Survivor

Because of the early and repeated childhood betrayals, and the fact that the true host and core and core splits will not present early in therapy, the survivor will be very untrusting, and unable to bond normally with, anyone who tries to help them. The most common presentation is "detached", since the parts that can attach are hidden very deeply within and are reserved for the primary programmer only.

While the survivor will not at first present as "needy", the attachment needs are still there, **and will drive recontact programming unless the survivor can learn to form healthy, safe attachments**. This will be the challenge for both the survivor, and their helpers, since the wounded, angry parts within will often test those they do bond with again and again, once they feel safe within the relationship.

Theta and spiritual attacks are difficult to bear for helpers, but the survivor will be completely unaware that they are occurring. Gently asking, or even confronting, the survivor with what is happening can help. They will need to learn to pray, and ask inside, to find out what is happening with the parts that they are not co-conscious with yet.

Once co-consciousness is established, and the parts come to Christ and the demonic is renounced, the warfare will usually diminish, much to the relief of the survivor and their helpers.

It will take all of the emotional resources the survivor has, as well as outside support, and a strong walk with Jesus, to face the original attachment pains that come up with remembering early childhood, infancy and prenatal events. This is when praying in the spirit, scripture study, journaling and talking with safe support can help tremendously as the survivor grieves the past, and begins to build a life based upon a new foundation.

Presenter programming is based on the **desire to "protect" these loved ones**

through either loyalty, or amnesia, or both.

The survivor who fears facing their past is one who fears betraying those they love; they are often "held hostage" through the group's control of or threatening to harm someone they love, whether a child, a mentee, a cult twin, or another relationship. To break free, the survivor must be shown, and truly believe, that only the LORD can rescue and keep safe these loved ones.

They must also be willing to count the cost of getting out, which is very high: no contact at all with former family, friends or loved ones, since they will all have been programmed to access the survivor. Few are willing to pay this price for freedom, and it is often the unconscious (unknown) love bonds that draw the survivor back in.

Chapter 6: Working with Healing Blockers

There is a specific set of cult loyal parts who have the job of blocking therapy. They do this in order to prevent the survivor from breaking their programming and becoming totally free of cult control, due to their fear that they will no longer be able to see their loved ones, or that their loved ones will be tortured.

Therapy blockers are highly programmed to completely resist therapy, and are extremely bonded to their trainers.

When a survivor of mind control enters therapy, these trainers will be notified (often by the survivor themselves, since they frequently "report in"), and specific programming to block therapy with their current therapist will begin to be put into place. This will be layered in over the generic "no heal" programming that all survivors have installed that prevents unauthorized system access, or any communication between presentation (front) parts and the cult host or systems.

Generic No Heal Programming

When the survivor is an infant, and child, they will be put through mock "therapy" sessions and deliverance sessions in which the "therapist" (a cult actor) kindly asks the child to share information and encourages them to disclose their abuse. Later in the setup, the child is then tortured for talking and disclosing, is raped by the mock therapist, and is "hospitalized" (see the section on Crazy Alice programming) to punish them for "making up" memories that "couldn't possibly be true". It is the brave survivor indeed who chooses to push past this programming to enter therapy at all, unless they have been sent on a mission for this purpose. In addition to the above, the survivor will see setups in which for every disclosure they make, a loved one is tortured horrifically, sending the message: "if you talk, your loved ones will be hurt." This basically shuts down healing for many.

More Specific Therapy Blocking Programming

Each therapist has an individual style of working with people, and this is often used against the survivor. Because most survivors are still cult active when they enter therapy, during "tune ups" (reprogramming sessions), the cult will attempt to make the survivor fear disclosure in therapy by doing the following:

- Create a VR of the therapist abusing the client following personal disclosure (shocks, rapes, etc.)

- Have an actor that looks similar to the therapist, trained to use the therapist's favorite phrases to encourage therapy, do mock therapy with the survivor. Each phrase used (over and over) is combined with shock, rape or other torture to the survivor, so when they hear it, they will recoil in pain and disgust.

- Mock therapy in which the survivor is programmed to only talk about certain issues, and they are heavily rewarded for doing so.

- Create a VR of the therapy room, and then have the "therapist" avatar perform rituals there, to convince the survivor that the therapist is "one of us" and therefore not safe to disclose to.

A survivor must overcome an enormous amount of pain and programming to trust a therapist at all, especially since during the time they still have contact with the cult, they and their loved ones will be tortured every time they attempt to heal during reprogramming sessions. If the survivor does choose to trust the therapist, they need to be aware that many people (but thankfully not all) drawn to providing therapy or support for DID, trauma, and ritual abuse are programmed cult members whose job is to access survivors seeking to get out. It is not unusual for the "supporter" to later discover that he/she is actually DID and programmed as well, as time goes on.

This is why choosing a therapist is a matter for prayer, discernment and seeking input from a safe person (if the therapist knows one) regarding who to see.

Because of the above programming, survivors will often attempt to block therapy using different methods. These fears are genuine, justified, and should not be minimized; instead, the survivor needs support and prayer from SAFE people as they work through the issues.

Typical Therapy Blocking Programs

When a therapist works with a survivor, they will see a lot of **ambivalence:** they want to heal, but part of them is avoiding the healing quite energetically. This can cause a lot of frustration in both the survivor, and the therapist, who over time may begin to wonder "Why don't you just heal???" The survivor will have tremendous internal conflicts between their entire worldview and experience, and the information that a therapist challenges this worldview with. In addition, the survivor will be emotionally invested in saving loved ones, who they believe are being tortured each time they break programming.

This ambivalence and internal conflict can cause the survivor to display any or all of the following programmed responses in therapy:

- **Cycling through over and over (rolodexing)**: this is a symptom of extreme system distress and conflict, as parts of the survivor are attempting to heal and incorporate new information, while other parts are terrified that the programming is breaking. This rapid switching is a sign that internal controllers are trying to stop doing their jobs (including hiding internal pain), are "failing", feeling terror and are attempting to send out a part to present unsuccessfully. Rolodexing can also be a punishment program that causes the survivor to look completely dysfunctional, and be used to reinforce the belief (which is a lie) that the survivor is "going insane", etc. Rolodexing will stop once the "hot topic" in therapy is dropped; this can be an opportunity to journal and work on the topic, since it is obviously important to healing or the system would not respond in this way.

- **Only one memory comes up:** some survivors go through weeks, months and even years processing only one or two memories that cycle through again and again, even though they recognize they were raised in a cult group. This is a way of blocking therapy, since the survivor never gets past that one memory to do other work inside.

- **House that Jack Built:** This is a specific form of blocking, in which the survivor cycles through bits and pieces of one memory, and each time, must repeat the same sequence in order before they can add new information to the memory. The survivor will appear to need to completely recount the previous information given before they can look at any new information regarding the memory, which can be wearing on both the survivor and therapist.

- **False Christian work**: If the survivor is working with a Christian therapist or deliverance ministry, they will pull out their false "god" "jesus" and "holy spirit" to "help" with the healing. They may be praying wholeheartedly, praying warfare prayers, doing daily Bible study, agreeing with the therapist, and reporting visions of "jesus" intervening inside and how "close" they feel to "god" during therapy. The problem is that they are not praying to the real Christian God who has the authority to heal, deliver and bring breakthrough, and this survivor will often leave therapy frustrated, wondering why God doesn't answer in spite of all the praying they are doing. This is heavily linked to anti-Christian programming (please see chapter on this topic).

- **False integrations**: If the survivor is on a mission to bond with the therapist, learn their techniques, and later report to the cult the therapy methods used, they will want the therapist to feel good about seeing them. This is often accomplished through false integrations, in which dozens, hundreds or more of parts are "miraculously joined together" without any trauma (or memories), and the survivor expresses deep gratitude about the "tremendous healing" they have received. This type of work can also be a response to a huge need to please a prayer or deliverance minister who pressures the survivor to integrate before they are ready. While God can and does the miraculous, most true integrations bring back life history, both good and bad, and resolve core conflicts and false beliefs that fueled the dissociation.

- **Therapy sabotage**: with this programming, the survivor will be late to appointments, may miss scheduled appointments, may "forget" to pay for therapy, does not do therapeutic homework, and verbalizes wanting to drop out. A subset of this program is distancing the therapist/supporter through methods such as pulling out sexual parts who attempt to "seduce" the therapist; pulling out hostile/rude/unpleasant parts who pick fights or tear the therapist down verbally, and even threaten to sue the therapist if they become desperate.

- **Shutdown programming:** At times, a survivor who is still in contact with the cult will be given a shutdown/stop healing command. When this is running, the survivor will experience the following:

    a. Is completely unable to communicate with parts inside

    b. Is unable to journal, collage or do artwork

    c. Feels intense anxiety at the thought of doing internal work

    d. Wants to be "normal" and "forget about healing", wants a "real life"

This form of programming is frustrating for both the survivor and therapist, since it seems to be a waste of therapy time working with someone who cannot communicate with parts. To resolve this, the survivor needs to look at where access occurred, how the shutdown command was given (including subliminals or texts online or by phone), and what threats were used to accomplish the shutdown (frequently, this will be a double bind being threatened).

- **Pulling out false issues to work on (cover issues):** It is common for survivors, especially early in their healing, to work on cover programming only to prevent their going deeper into their system. The survivor may only remember their American host family; or believe that they were only sexually abused, or abused by an organized cult group for a few years, then "let go when they moved away from home" or "married someone outside the group" (which almost never happens in reality).

  The more sophisticated groups may create a whole cover for their agents, such as believing they were raised in the Templar Knights (which was true for these parts – they were actually hosted by a Templar family), while in reality they were raised and programmed during earliest childhood by a different organization, and programmed to infiltrate the Templars. Until the survivor goes past the cover, and is able to work with the true programming and beliefs that run the system, healing will be sporadic and difficult, and they will be vulnerable to reaccess.

The survivor must be willing to pray, fast and go deep inside, journaling and asking the LORD to uncover the truth, regardless of what it is. They must be willing to go "all out" for the LORD, and trust their loved ones in the group to His care, as they go past guardians, system blocks, demonic blocks and learn what is actually inside.

- **Doubt: Belief that the survivor will never heal**: This is programming designed to knock out the effectiveness of prayer by the survivor and therapist/supporter. This programming will be installed with setups in which the child is told to "heal" or "break the programming" under command – and then experiences horrendous pain and terror (through VR or tech torture). The child in numerous setups is told to "integrate" and again, pain, terror and hopelessness is installed. This is layered in many times over the years. When the survivor does try to heal in therapy, they will often re-experience these feelings of pain, hopelessness and futility regarding healing, or even the possibility of God answering their prayers (see anti-Christian programming for more information on this).

  The survivor will also have been shown videos of individuals in lab settings attempting to break the programming that was installed in them – and the people viewed go insane, or die. They will be shown the readouts for their slow, agonizing death, to instill the belief that the programming can never be broken. **In actuality, if that was really true, the programmers would not have to install this false belief**. It can help the survivor to understand that their situation is different: unlike the individuals they watched trying to break programming in a facility dedicated to demons, the survivor has a God that loves them and can heal anything, safety, and support that the people they watched did not have.

- **Emotional flooding that does not promote healing**: Some survivors will present in therapy appearing to be willing to heal, but the instant that any memory comes forward, they will burst into tears and appear to "melt down" for what can amount to the entire therapy session, wailing over their guilt and self-condemnation. While emotions will come with the recall of traumatic memories (and should), seeing hours of therapy "hijacked" by a part crying every time the survivor comes to therapy could be a sign that this is running.

  The supporter or therapist may want to gently confront or challenge this part regarding their job within the system, and see if the survivor is willing to work past this program. The survivor will need to become aware if it is running, and break any agreements to have this part step forward if anything is disclosed. The traumas that created this response will also need to be resolved.

- **Child presentation**: Normally, the infants and children in a mind-controlled system are heavily protected and guarded, and do not come out in therapy until trust and safety have been established over time. A completely young presentation is highly abnormal, and can be the result of several things:

  a. Programming breakdown: some survivors literally "burn out", especially if they have been heavily used in the field on missions, and too much "wipe out" and other amnesia programming of presenters afterwards can cause a situation in which the adults are too tired/traumatized to present, and children come forward

  b. Mission programming: some survivors are programmed to present with children in order to seem "harmless" and "cute" as they infiltrate a church or therapy organization. This is a programmed-in presentation, with great trauma.

  c. Secondary reward: some systems have been heavily rewarded by abusers for "staying young" and childlike, especially if the main abuser was a pedophile. The survivor may have starved themselves as a child/teen in order to prevent the appearance of breasts and delay the onset of menses, and to keep their childlike physical appearance. This is often a system highly dependent upon others, and they may look to therapists and supporters to "caretake" them as an adult.

- **Constant crises with no resolution (burn out the support):** This is vicious programming, because the survivor has no idea that this is happening. All they know is that they are in deep distress, and want to pick up the phone and call the only person that can help them (the therapist or support person). There will be crises during the healing journey; but a life of constantly cycling into crisis could be an indication that something is wrong. This type of programming is designed to "burn out" the supporter, who becomes exhausted helping someone who never heals.

- **Denial:** Every survivor will have some form of denial programming, and parts inside will hold this job. Denial parts are among the most cult loyal, and deeply fear the torture or death of loved ones (including trainers) in the cult. Denial parts will often verbalize the following:

  a. It wasn't that bad

  b. I'm exaggerating things

  c. I'm making this up; I have a creative, sick imagination

  d. I'm not dissociative

  e. I'm just seeking attention

f. This is all for secondary gain; I've been playing with your head

g. I'm a liar

This part will have been heavily programmed since the survivor was in the womb to say these things – and believe them. They are part of the primary amnesia triad for presentations (denial, doubt and despair) that keep the survivor from truly believing their own memories. Healing of denial means finding why these parts (often represented in numerous systems) are so invested in doing their job, i.e. who they are protecting, and why. They will be heavily bonded to a primary bond, and thus will be unwilling (or unable, due to amnesia agreements) to disclose who they are protecting until safety and trust are established with the supporter, and with the true God.

Chapter 7: Antichristian Programming

Because real Christianity is such a threat to cult groups, since it brings faith, love and healing (and therefore, rapid program degradation), they go to extensive lengths to program in false Christianity in the hopes that the individual will never come to a true faith in Christ. This programming is started in the womb, with numerous setups conducted with the birth mother and fetus to begin turning the fetus's heart away from God – and towards Satan.

In a typical setup, an actor dressed as "Jesus" and proclaiming that he is the "son of god", etc. will rape and torture the birth mother, telling her "This is how I show my love for you" and other scripts. The fetus hears and feels the mother's distress, and incorporates the hatred for this "Jesus" that the birth mother feels.

In other setups, the birth mother is tortured, and told to pray to God for help. As she does so, the pain is increased, and continues to do so, until she stops praying, and then "Satan" "rescues" the birth mother and fetus from the pain.

In still other setups, the fetus will see a bright light (held against the abdominal walls) and a voice telling the fetus, "I am God, and I hate you" as electrical shocks are administered. Other similar setups are done, including rape by 'Jesus' of the fetus (with a Q-Tip like instrument inserted into the womb). A false "holy spirit" will descend as well, offering the "way out of the pain."

Once the infant is born, the programming continues, with actors dressed as "Jesus", "the disciples", "Mary" and other biblical figures talking to the infant, abusing the infant, or comforting, depending upon the role. There will usually be two types of "Jesus" portrayed: a punishing, angry, wrathful God and Jesus for the black or cult systems; and a loving, caring, kind "Jesus" portrayed for the white systems, since the programming allows for two paths for ascension: the black path (satanic) and the white path (false Christianity). The presentations are heavily programmed to stay on the "white path" and never stray, or terrible things (abuse, pain) occur. Within the systems, a part called "god" is the judge and metes out punishments or rewards depending upon how well the controllers and parts obey cult directives and rules.

As the child becomes older, the setups become more elaborate; there will be setups in which "Jesus and disciples" are "fishing for men", the child is invited onto the boat, where the nauseating stench of rotten fish fills the boat; the child is repeatedly raped and abused by the false Jesus and disciples, who smell like rotten fish, as they repeatedly tell the child to "become a fisher of men" as they are. This will cause severe nausea and repugnance at the thought of Christianity later in life in the parts that underwent this abuse.

Almost every significant scripture in the New Testament, and many in the Old Testament, are used during these abuse scenarios, causing the parts to eventually recoil in pain, horror and disgust at any mention of Christianity or scripture. This is all hidden in the subconscious; the survivor will have no conscious recall of these memories, and will only know a deep unease and guilt at being unable to enjoy church or sit through a sermon.

Cruz (the cross) is a figure in some groups who exhorts the presentation to stay on the "white path" (cult false Christianity) and to "take up the cross and follow me." This is a form of false guilt in which the presenters attempt to be their own messiah, or to rescue others, by staying perfectly on the demanding and rigid white path of false Christianity.

Elaborate setups are done with a fake "church" or "bible study" in which the child being programmed goes to church, where the members all then turn on her and abuse her, all the time using Christian phrases, or attempting the "laying on of hands" and "imparting the holy spirit" to her. This is to create a barrier between internal parts and hearing the gospel, which to them means abuse.

Fake witch trials and burning at the stake will be done by "Christians" to cult and spiritual parts, to convince them to hate Christians. "Christians" (cult actors) will come into the nurseries and abuse screaming babies, laughing at their pain as they rape with crucifixes, telling the babies they are showing them the "love of god."

During yearly events, the higher occultic groups will have events at which real Christians are brought to and tortured or crucified (such as the infamous "Roman games" held each year). These Christians are rounded up from prisons and camps in third world countries under oppressive regimes, and are the main event for one reason alone: Satan hates Christians and Christianity, and takes every chance possible to persecute and kill them.

Children may be forced as part of their "God can never forgive you" programming (meant to create a barrier of guilt between them and God) to wipe out Christian villages in third world countries; or to abduct and sell the children of Christians, or infiltrate Christian churches and seduce the leadership (or their children).

If a member of these groups becomes a real Christian, then there will be extensive programming to destroy the individual's faith. They will be labeled a "traitor" and an "adulterer" or "whore" because they chose Christianity over the group's beliefs (Satan), and the group will go to great lengths to get the new believer to recant. This may include:

- Placing the individual on a cross for days, as they are intermittently raped and tortured. They are told the torture will stop if they recant
- Torturing the individual's brothers and sisters to death in front of them, one by one, telling them the killing will only stop if they recant

- If older, killing the individual's husband and children in various presentations may be done to get them to recant
- Placing them in a room with a false "Jesus" for weeks who abuses and tortures them and tells them he hates them, every time they pray
- Raping the individual with dogs, horses and corpses, with the same message
- Bringing the individual into a room filled with children on crosses, and being told they will all die unless the individual recants.

In circumstances like the above, the individual will eventually be driven to their limit (sometimes after weeks of continuous torture). They will then recant, not from a loss of faith, but sheer emotional exhaustion and overload, and the inability to see more death of loved ones. Once the person recants, the programming to ensure that they believe they can never "come back to God" will start almost immediately. A false "god" and "Jesus", angry and horrified in the setup, will condemn the individual to "hell" for "giving up their faith" in very cruel setups. They will be forced to sacrifice and renew their vows to Satan and the antichrist.

The individual will be forced to torture a Christian to death, and be told, "Now, the Christian God can never forgive you." They will be sent on antichristian missions as described above, to seal the programming.

Can God forgive the believer who recants under weeks of torture such as described above? I believe He does, because He is merciful. The Bible states that if any man sins, we have an advocate with God – His son, Jesus. If anyone confesses their sin, they are forgiven. Recalling memories of torture and recanting can be extremely distressing. It can cause deep guilt and grief. It is important that the survivor comes to realize that there is no sin that God cannot and will not forgive, if they come to Him and ask forgiveness. God knew all of our sins, both past, present and future, when we first came to faith in Him. Nothing in the survivor's life shocks or horrifies Him. Instead, He offers forgiveness for the very worst that mankind can do, against one another, and Himself, because He paid the price in full on the cross.

Chapter 8: Working with Cult Loyal Parts

Without the eventual help of cult loyal parts, the survivor will not be able to break free of the cult. These parts hold a great deal of power in the system, and will include the cult host, internalized leadership councils, and people the survivor loves most on this earth.
The problem with healing for many survivors is based upon this reality. It is often a presenter who enters therapy, due to depression, feeling that "something isn't quite right", cutting, an eating disorder, etc. While the presenter's needs are real, they will have made extensive agreements (during rituals, sacrifices, participating in covenants with demons and loved ones) to never remember their cult abuse, on pain of the death of their loved ones. This means that the presenter who presents in therapy is already heavily invested in never remembering the abuse – and will have extensive amnesia.

If only the presenter(s) appears in therapy, then the amount of healing that can occur will be limited to the presenters.

For deeper healing, word needs to get out to the inner, hidden parts (often called 'back parts", "dark parts", "cult parts") that they can get free – and they need to want this and begin to believe it is possible. This is so important because it is often these parts that run the show for the survivor and during therapy; presenters and other parts will often refer to them as "the bosses", "scary parts", "trainers", "leaders", etc. They have the power within the system to initiate punishment programs to prevent healing (and do), and to either help or hinder healing. The survivor will need support in order to patiently love, communicate with and listen to these parts, because there will be large amounts of programming installed to prevent exactly that. If a "back part" pops out and makes a rude comment, the presentation will be programmed to be absolutely horrified. If parts share about the individual's cult life, the presentation will have been programmed to deny everything, or to believe that they cannot handle hearing about the abuse (which is not true).

Attachment, Bonding and Cult Loyalty

The cult develops loyalty in its members through love bonds. While most books about cults stress the horrific nature of the abuse (and it is), few mention the deep love bonds that develop between members of the group. This bonding is developed in infancy through the manipulation of the infant's attachment needs: the primary trainers will change, rock, soothe and give bottles to the infant, talk lovingly, in order to teach the infant to love them. Since this is the only positive interaction the infant experiences when growing up in a cult facility, the infant will bond deeply to these programmers.

When a survivor enters therapy, and tries to break free, they must break these attachment bonds with the people they love most, or they will be drawn back into the cult. This creates deep psychological conflict for the individual who simultaneously wants out, wants the abuse to stop, and wants to stop abusing others; but who must cut off all contact with dearly loved ones in order to do so.

Cult programmers purposely keep young parts young, in order to continue manipulating attachment bonds for greater control. Breaking these bonds can be incredibly difficult, as the younger parts in the survivor will become angry and upset about not seeing the people they love. These littles are often bonded to a cult "mama" and "papa" who even when they are adults rock them, soothe them, sing to them, and give them candy or bottles. This type of treatment is provided after every programming session, in order to reinforce the bonding to the programmer(s). As the survivor tries to break free, angry littles will come out and say "I want my mama (or papa)" and refuse to have anything to do with anyone else. Young parts who miss beloved adults may hit or yell at support people, blaming these supporters for the fact that the survivor is unable to see the people they are bonded to.

It is important that these younger parts have a healthy, non-dissociative adult and support in their lives that they can bond to. Introducing them to the real Jesus is also helpful, since it will cause them to hesitate to recontact individuals who hate Christianity and Christians, and provides a source of love to attach to.

The number one reason that survivors go back to the cult is the lack of safe support to attach to as they leave the group. The cult loyal parts inside basically think "Why should I give up everyone I love, to live all alone, with no one to love me?" Therapy can be helpful, but traditional therapy is normally one hour a week, which will not offset a lifetime of cult bonding. This is why safe support is so critical for survivors, and is their biggest need. With support, the survivor can tackle the emotional tasks required for healing, including detaching from their abusers.

Cult loyal parts often get a bad "rap" from survivors and others, since they seem to create a lot of "problems". But given safety, support and the chance to receive truth, they will become the greatest force for healing inside, as their deep love and loyalty move from the cult to the Christian God and safe support. These parts, especially the cult host and the core controlling systems, will know the survivor's entire life history and can help keep the survivor safe from access. They will instantly recognize individuals from the cult, can warn the survivor of danger, and will often have a very strong faith and prayer life once they become Christians.

Internalized Loved Ones

When the infant is tiny (or even still in the womb) they will be asked to receive a familiar spirit from loved ones (such as their twin or triplet; their favorite trainers, etc.) They will be told that by receiving the spirit, the loved one can "always be with you" and the infant/child will "never be alone." Fearing abandonment, this sounds good to the child and they agree. This is accomplished through rituals that can include sexual activity, being put to death and resurrected together, or exchanging blood. The familiar spirit is a spirit of delusion that makes the infant/child/adult believe that the internal part is actually the outside loved person.

These internal representations of loved ones are used to control the survivor in various ways.

- If the survivor disobeys the cult, this internal part may be tortured, fulfilling the promise that if the survivor tries to leave or heal, their loved ones will be tortured or killed
- The internal part often holds great control over programming, reprogramming and amnesia systems
- The internal part may seek spiritual (astral) recontact with the loved person if physical access is stopped
- The internal part may be programmed to beg the survivor to "save them" (with tears and cries of pain) by going back to the group, if the survivor tries to break off cult contact.

It is important that the internal parts receive deliverance from the delusional (familiar) spirits and that the original identity of the part is restored, through prayer. The survivor will need to work with these parts, letting them know that they are programmed parts, and are actually part of the survivor and not the outside person. Allowing these parts out to experience current reality can help with grounding them, and bringing truth to them can help them choose to stop doing their old jobs inside.

Children are often programmed in groups of 12 (graded for performance so that individuals of similar ability are programmed together), and view this cohort as their siblings, since they have been raised together and done everything together since earliest infancy. They will have internal representations of these individuals they have closely bonded to internally, and will have great difficulty breaking bonds with these beloved peers. The survivor will need support in grieving the loss when they choose to leave the group, since the friendships and camaraderie experienced on the battlefield and during training and school are deep indeed.

Leadership Councils

The survivor's inside world will reflect the outside world they were raised in. If they were raised in a cult facility, there will be an internal one. If they lived under a cult council's leadership, there will be one internally. There will be internal trainers; internal training rooms and labs; council rooms, and mage councils. The cult hierarchy will be reflected in the individual's system, with the top leaders representing "ascended" or "celestial" beings who have overcome "human mortality."

These parts are heavily invested in the beliefs of the group regarding heaven, hell and ascension. They will believe that all of the torture and abuse they have undergone will be rewarded in a celestial paradise filled with good food, heavenly music, angels and good things. These constructs are installed in infancy, with elaborate staging and actors playing out the roles.

Core Loyalty

The highest parts of a system will be the darkest and most dissociated. Around the core, there may be a deep hatred of all mankind and humanity, with the vow (made in the womb, during prenatal torture) to get revenge on the abusers of the fetus and birth mother (see core programming). The fetus will have agreed to allow Satan (or a spirit representing him) to enter in after extreme trauma, because this spirit promises the fetus that it will help him/her become powerful, and one day wreak revenge on all mankind.

An internal "Satan" will be one of the first core splits (this will also be replicated with a Satan in all the other systems as a major controller), and the child will be highly loyal to him due to this desire for revenge. An internal "god" will also be a primary core split. These first core splits are heavily rewarded, praised and doted on, and will have bonded to the demonic (and in fact, may have had no interaction with human beings). Breaking loyalty at this level involves forgiving the abusers in the womb (by the fetal splits) and forgiving God, since the fetus blames God for the abuse.

Anti-Traitor/Anti-Stranger Programming

All cult groups fear and hate traitors, or members who try to leave, as well as "strangers" or non-cult members. This is reinforced with extensive programming, starting in the womb. A "traitor" will enter the room the birth mother is in, and painfully rape and torture her, telling her "this is what traitors do." This instills in the fetus a deep subconscious hatred of traitors. During infancy, this setup is repeated, with the infant tortured and raped by actors who come into the nursery saying scripts such as "I'm a traitor and I want you to be one too". The traitors smell awful, and the infant is repulsed by the foul smell and abuse, until they are "saved" by the primary programmer(s) who tell them to stay away from traitors.

As the child gets older, the setups become more sophisticated. The child may be "abducted" by traitors, who horrifically abuse the child until the child can escape or is "rescued" in the setup. During military camp training, the child may be captured by "traitors" and interrogated under torture; the child is extensively praised for not disclosing any information. The child is taught to avoid traitors and strangers, with abductions by strangers in setups where the child is raped and abused continuously until they are able to escape and go back to those who "love" them at the facility: their programmers and siblings.

These parts who have been extensively programmed to hate outsiders, and hate themselves if they leave the group, will initially be horrified and angry at the choice to leave. They may act out on self harm and suicide programming, preferring death to life as a traitor. They may attempt to sabotage therapy and support, and will call supporters names (such as "traitor enabler" and worse). It takes time, patience and bringing truth to these parts, and a safe, non-abusive attachment figure for these often young parts to realize that they were lied to.

Twin and Triplet Bonding

Most modern sophisticated groups that use mind control will produce their members through genetic manipulation. The state of genetic engineering is far beyond what the public realizes, and traits such as intelligence, strength, muscle mass, healing ability and pain endurance, spiritual/psychic ability, as well as phenotypes such as hair color and eye color, have been genetically engineered for many decades. G1 was the first group of genetically enhanced individuals produced (in the late 1940's), G3 (Generation 3) appeared in the late 1950's, G13 was produced in the mid-1990's and today I would guess it is near G20. The genes and DNA can be purchased by smaller groups from the larger genetic labs; the largest (and wealthiest) groups have their own genetic labs. Once a new generation is produced, the birth mothers are implanted with multiple zygotes. Only one per birth mother (the strongest) will be allowed to live, but there will be several gene-identical individuals produced who are carried by their own birth mothers. In this manner, identical twins and triplets are produced who were carried in different wombs. These twins and triplets are allowed to bond deeply throughout life, and will often become the deepest love bonds for the individual.

Twins (or triplets) will undergo numerous scenarios in which they "rescue" each other, undergo torture for one another, or even agree to be put to death for the other (and are subsequently resuscitated). This creates a very deep bond. They may be placed with one another in cribs in infancy, and undergo early programming within sight of each other, and be allowed to comfort each other after the programming sessions are over. If an infant becomes a "failure to thrive" (which is very common due to the terrible abuse during the first year) they will be allowed to spend extra time with their twin sibling(s), in order to help restore the will to live. They will be told "Your twin needs you to live or she will have to take all the pain alone" or "Your twin needs your protection or she might die" etc.

Breaking this deep emotional and spiritual bond is difficult, since this is one of the closest relationships the survivor was allowed when growing up. It requires support, understanding and the chance to grieve the loss if there is no contact with the siblings. In most instances, these twin/triplets who are still in the group will be threatened with torture, causing great distress in the survivor who must come to realize that she/he can NOT be a "messiah" or rescue their siblings; that only the Christian God is powerful enough to do so.

Antichrist Programming

One of the deepest loyalty programs within an occultic system will be to the New World Order and the promised "messiah" or the individual the Bible refers to as the "antichrist" (the occultic groups look to him as a savior and leader who will usher in peace and prosperity). The antichrist is referred to by occultic groups as the "Light of the World" (which is also the name of a famous occultic painting created in the mid-1800's which depicts the antichrist leading the world and men of all races looking towards him).

Antichrist programming in many systems was formerly represented by silvery blue, but since 2000 has been represented by the colors white and gold. Many groups believe that this individual was born in 2000, and will rise to power in the year 2030 (this cannot be verified, since the Christian God is the one in charge of history and is in control of world events). The antichrist represented internally will be a high controller (normally, of the core system), and will rule over the internal celestial city, which is the occultic form to the "new Jerusalem". This internal celestial city will have a tree of life in its center; a central fountain of life and "living waters" and will have internal alters (for sacrifices). This system will be built upon numerous sacrifices, and will often be quite disconnected from normal emotions or conscience; instead, the "ascended beings" that inhabit it will be in a state of bliss and peace. They will be completely loyal and bonded to the antichrist (called "he who has come") and will have made vows to serve him. Breaking this programming and the associated bonding and loyalty vows will create spiritual warfare, and requires prayer (and possibly fasting) and support to completely break the loyalty programming.

Chapter 9: Helping Spiritual Systems Heal

When survivors choose to heal, they will eventually meet their internal spiritual parts, which reside within specific systems and structures. These will vary with different groups, but will have the following traits in common:

1. Rituals are done before the programming, during and after the session (including sacrifices).
2. The spiritual parts will be committed to a deity, or believe they are the deity. This is accomplished by having the "deity" (an actor) introduce themselves to the survivor in the womb. After birth, actors dressed up as the deity demonstrate how the part is to walk, talk and act; and perform sacrifices in front of the infant. After sexual abuse with the actor, the demonic spirit then enters the infant. The part that the demon attaches to then believes that they are the entity.
3. This programming is reinforced heavily during early childhood, with role plays, VRs and other setups. This is one reason why international groups prefer to program their infants and children fulltime in facilities (with breaks of a few weeks each year to be hosted by presentation families): it can take years to install and reinforce these structured systems internally.

Theta Spiritual Systems

Theta is a brain wave state that is highly sensitive to the spiritual. When in theta state, a person can more easily see spiritual beings and under their influence, can experience greatly enhanced abilities (such as being able to run at superfast speeds, leap extremely high, and have extremely enhanced eyesight and hearing). Theta state is also used to create parts with specific spiritual roles, which include:

- Theta remote viewing (the ability to leave the body, and enter a building remotely and share information regarding what is seen there),
- Theta killing: these assassins are trained from the time they are in the womb to kill psychically; normally, after a sexual union with the victim. The theta will be sent to have sexual intercourse with the victim, create a soul tie, and later use the soul tie to kill the person demonically. At times, teams of thetas will join together to kill individuals with a strong will to live or who have strong demonic protection themselves.
- Astral communication: thetas can communicate with other thetas by astral projection or

inter-psychically.

Thetas can be trained to send the following to others:

- Tremendous fear (Phobos): this includes sending dreams of death or terror
- Death (Thanatos): this is the root of psychic killing
- Revenge: (Nemesis): normally a strong theta controller, Nemesis represents the desire to wreak revenge on mankind (for its mortality) and to destroy others.

Omicron and Mu

These are extremely high and low brain wave states used to increase the receptivity to spiritual attachments. Omicron is extremely painful to maintain and can lead to a death state quickly; and is considered a doorway to meeting "spiritual beings" or "enlightened beings" (which are actually demons). Mu is an extremely low brain wave state (near death) which again allows the demonic easier entrance. It is often used in conjunction with other programming.

Omega Programming

Omega programming is spiritual programming that enhances oracle and mage skills and abilities (mages are occultic practitioners who are skilled in casting spells and power battles). This is also the state in which complete system destruction sequences are often placed. This system believes it is highly evolved and "ascended" and does not feel the body or mortality. It will be heavily programmed with deep loyalty to the group and trainers, and will be programmed to die or cause system shatter if the survivor seriously disobeys cult commands and becomes a security risk. The survivor may literally attempt to "implode" with this programming, and will need support to work through it.

Omega skills are also used to take on the pain for others, such as when a woman is carrying a hybrid (half human, half demonic) child, since this type of pregnancy causes intense torment (and at times, even death) in the carrier. An omega team will help carry the demonic torment, allowing the pregnancy to continue without spiritually destroying the birth mother.

Ancient Spiritual Systems

There are numerous ancient spiritual systems that Occultic groups draw from in their spiritual programming. Some include:

- **The Garden of Eden (biblical)**: the core may reside in this garden setting, which is also inhabited by Lilith, Adam, Eve, the snake and is often where the core resides, insulated from any interaction with outside life. Inside of Eden will be the following structures:

- The Tree of Life (althea, representing satanic immortality), the Tree of the Knowledge of Good and Evil (false, human logic), and Cruz (the cross, representing false Christianity). These three twine together and run through all systems as a three-fold cord of false logic and belief
- A waterfall
- Benches where the core meets with Satan ("god" in the system) for counsel
- Flaming cherubim (system barrier preventing crossing outside without authorization, or entrance)
- A recreation of the temple in Jerusalem, with alters for sacrifice and a "holy of holies"

- **Babylonian**

  Many Occultic groups have access to the scrolls and tablets written by Babylonian mages and wise men (or at least copies), which describe dimensional travel, rituals, shape shifting and other forms of demonic activity. The internal controllers will have the names of Babylonian deities (such as Bel, Ishtar, Ashtoth, etc.) and will have undergone Babylonian pain rituals (golden needles heated and inserted into 1000 nerve points, while the person is suspended), and other forms of training (such as learning to "pass through the fire" in a golden chair without being burned alive).

  The mage craft taught includes how to read magic books (where the pages come alive), how to play demonic chess (with the chess "master" learning how to control the white, and then the black pieces, which become demonically alive). Learning to shape shift (take on the form of a bird or wolf) is rooted in Babylonian mage craft, and students learn the required rituals (that often include learning to create the circles or geometric figures with great care) from mentors, or spiritual "masters".

  The Babylonian parts will often reside in ziggurats or a recreation of a babylonian temple inside.

- **Egyptian Programming**

  This is similar in some ways to Babylonian programming, but involves the major Egyptian deities (Ra, Isis, Osiris, Horus, etc.). The child will be taken to a recreation of an Egyptian temple, or to the chambers below a great pyramid, where sacrifices are done. The young child is often chained to a statue representing a deity with an attached alter, and left overnight; if the child lives and is not killed demonically, they will have internalized the deity whose statue they were chained to.

These demons often can create great torment for the survivor and others, with parts able to call up clouds of swarming, stinging bees or gnats, or other curses. Helping them involves getting rid of the demonic, breaking soul ties to the human mentor and the demonic, and helping these parts realize that they are part of a human being. Because the demonic pretended to "protect" them for years, giving up the demonic may make the survivor feel vulnerable, until they have learned that the Christian God actually gives greater protection, and without the terrible price that demons exact.

- **Indian/Tibetan and Asian**
  Most international groups ensure that the individuals they program take part in knowledge gathered from religions around the world. They will be required to learn Sanskrit (which has many ancient rituals described), and other ancient languages, and those well-versed will even converse in these languages. They may meet the "living Buddha" and offer him reverence and sacrifice; and gain demonic power from a large variety of sources. When learning martial arts, they will learn to channel "chi" and other forms of demonic power to do the seemingly impossible feats and enhance their own combat skills.

- **Q'bala**
  I have addressed the Q'bala in earlier writings. A Jewish form of mysticism, it is used to open up portals for dimensional travel at the points of the sephiroth (i.e. installation of demons). It also drives part of the logic for the delta system, and the tree of life runs through it.

- **Druids**
  Druids are considered the "tree huggers" of the Occultic world, but they have powerful blood rituals based upon human sacrifice that are far from gentle or kind. The Druid Council runs the U.K., and druids are adept at shapeshifting (into animal or tree form). Druid rituals often involve a child being chained to a tree (large oak) under which sacrifices have been performed, and the tree then rapes and demonically speaks to the child at night.

- **Witches, Mages and Warlocks**
  These are all different branches of Occultic learning which members of groups go through, with mages considered the most learned of the three (and the most powerful). Mages will often engage in power battles, and spend years mentoring their students in the Occultic rituals required. Mages can also shapeshift (into birds, ravens, or mage wolves), and can send powerful curses, and the most powerful mages will be part of a mage council over an area. Fortunately, the Christian God is able to stop all curses and protect those who turn to His protection, and who renounce all forms of witchcraft, sorcery or mage craft.

- **Ascended Masters**

  These are considered the highest individuals in the Occultic world, who have passed through horrendous death rituals and have basically "overcome" their "human mortality" through pain that would cause shock and death to those who have not undergone training to endure it; they have also often traveled to the highest dimensions (12th and 13th) in their quest for "enlightenment."

  Basically, these individuals have given over their hearts, minds and souls to be possessed demonically, and use these demonic powers to further the goals of the New World Order and usher in the reign of the antichrist. They will be familiar with working with nephilim and with the satanic agenda to destroy mankind, and will agree with it.

- **Demonic parts (Janus, Guardians, Dark Cherubim, shadows, wraiths, residents of hell)**

The survivor of international Occultic abuse will have numerous parts inside that have been programmed to believe that they are "demons". These are often young children (ages 1-4) that were taught to act like demons, growl, and given demonic names. The actors who model how to be a "demon" to the child will act in every way as if they are the demon.

  - Janus will be a demonic entity who appears like the Greek Janus, with two faces, one facing inwards (the dark face) and one facing outwards (the white face). Janus acts as a guardian between front and back, along a large porticullis (gate) that separates the two. Both aspects of Janus will need healing and deliverance, since her job was to prevent unauthorized passing back and forth between front and back.

  - Guardians: these will sound like demons and are actually protectors that guard infants, small children, or high-security areas inside. They will attempt to block the survivor or therapists from gaining access until convinced that allowing them in is helpful. It can help if these parts can share how they got their jobs and why they do them, as well as get rid of the demonic attachments that sit on them.

  - Dark Cherubim and angels: most spiritual systems will have a light (white) side, of false Christianity that includes false angels; in the same way, the dark system will have its counterparts, including dark angels, Princes of Hell, Generals of Hell and other parts. Again, these parts have been programmed both prenatally and during early infancy with role models, actors and VRs. Dismantling this is a combination of spiritual deliverance and looking at the setups that created the beliefs.

  - Shadows and wraiths: these are ethereal beings without physical body that have been created through spiritual torture; they may also be "modeled" through movies and VRs to create the internal counterpart. These parts often "follow" and track victims, working with the thetas to search and find those they are to torment or kill.

- Residents of hell: these are parts that were created to inhabit the various layers of hell internally, and will appear like demons, archangels, or other spiritual beings (see punishment programming chapter for more information).

- **Celestials**

The satanic counterpart of the Christian heaven is "celestial City" and paradise. This is an area where parts who believe they are "ascended beings" who have overcome "mortality" inhabit; and represent the reward for those who help bring in the New World Order.

Celestial City and its counterparts are installed through rituals and large numbers of sacrifices; and the inhabitants will have undergone so much torture and pain that they have completely dissociated their feelings. In the VRs of Celestial City, the inhabitants are programmed with drugs or brain stimulation to feel peace and bliss. These parts will come out declaring great peace and no fear of death (they have all undergone death and "resurrection" within the city) and believe they have "ascended" beyond earthy desires or needs. There is a huge spirit of deception and delusion that must be dealt with, and doing so will cause great anger when the parts realize that they have been deceived, and given their lives and sweat to a lie.

With time, and the chance to grieve, and with faith in the true God, these parts can heal and help the other parts in their healing journey. This takes time, since they have a lifetime of false teaching to work through. They will need time and patience to connect with the other systems, and realize that they are part of a human being.

- **Satan**

In all occultic systems, Satan (and his representative on earth, the antichrist) will hold primary positions, and will often be among the first core split(s). In many systems, Satan will have his black (punishing) form, and his kind (Lucient) form, with splits for each. The system will often perform sacrifices internally around the clock to the internal Satan, antichrist, and other deities, without the survivor's conscious knowledge. This can create a tremendous struggle internally, until the sacrifices, hymns of praise and other forms of worship internally stop as the individual begins to allow truth to replace the lies they were raised with.

As the primary punisher, the internal Satan will sit on his throne, and mete out judgments internally (or rewards) based upon behavior and obedience to cult laws and rules. If the individual obeys, they are rewarded (and ascend, enjoying internal bliss and peace); if they disobey, they are punished, and parts will begin descending in the internal "hell" until they "repent" or begin obeying again. The satanic systems will believe as fully that they are going to heaven, and that disobeying cult rules is sending them to hell, as the Christian systems believe in the Christian God and heaven. This can create a great deal of conflict during healing, until the satanic/luciferian systems come to recognize the truth of the Bible, and see how they have been lied to and manipulated by their abusers.

This will cause a great deal of grief. Often, the core is completely bonded to Satan, loves him, and wants to obey him, looking to him as their "father" figure; breaking this bond and the hold that Satan has on the system requires re-bonding to someone who is safe, and learning the truth about Jesus. This part of the system will often be the most hidden and invested in blocking healing, since undoing spiritual programming at this level will often allow massive healing of other systems.

Chapter 10: Helping Littles and Infants Heal

For the survivor to heal, their younger parts (child, toddler, infant and fetal) must also heal. These parts, often called "littles" by survivors, hold a lot of emotional power within the system. Their emotional needs are often what drives recontact programming, and should never be ignored.

The Need for Attachment

One of the greatest needs that littles have is to have a safe attachment figure. If they are not allowed to attach to a safe, non-cult person, their emotional needs will continue to drive them back to loved ones in the cult, where this need will be met.

All programmers understand attachment needs; after every programming session, the programmer will spend time with the infant and young parts inside, holding them, rocking them, giving them bottles and speaking lovingly to them. They realize the powerful emotions that these parts hold, and how important to keeping the programming intact these attachment needs are.

Breaking programming always involves breaking attachments to unsafe (cult) people that the survivor loves. This is one of the most difficult emotional tasks the survivor will ever have to do, and one of the most important for healing. To break attachments to unsafe people, a safe alternative must be presented. While it would be nice to be able to pat the survivor on the back, and tell him/her to "let Jesus be the one you bond to" this is not enough. The survivor was wounded in relationship with a human being, and needs to heal in relationship with one. Offering less is an emotional "copout" but is one that many therapists and supporters take.

Littles will often be direct about their attachment needs. They will ask to be held, rocked, and comforted. The nature of the support relationship will determine the boundaries to be held, but at the very least, the supporter can let the littles know they are cared for, and be given the smiles and looks of "delight" that infants and young children crave. This can promote healing faster than any other intervention offered, since it is attachments to cult people that draw the survivor back.

Guardians and Protectors

Littles and infants will often have highly protective guardians and protectors placed over them, whose job is to ensure that the littles never come out unless called out. Infants are often called out with a special "love name" given them by the trainers. Using this name causes them to immediately come out, expecting treats, petting and loving care.

The guardians and protectors are heavily punished throughout infancy and childhood, until they learn their job and do it well, keeping the infants inside. This is why in most systems with mind control, the littles and infants are never seen in therapy, until a lot of trust has been established over time. It often takes years of trust building with a safe person until these young parts are willing to test the waters and come out.

Systems that do not guard their infants and littles may do so because of complete presentation breakdown (no adults present to protect), or because the group was unsophisticated and heavily rewarded the individual for appearing young and childlike.

In many systems, there is a special guardian such as "Pan" who plays his pipes, and calls the littles to follow after him. He takes them to a special play area, with carousels and fun things to do, which keeps the littles entertained inside – and not presenting. In order to help the littles heal, the help of Pan and other similar guardians needs to be enlisted. Otherwise, the littles will be kept away from therapy, and healing.

Internal Playlands

There are other internal playlands for littles as well. Never-Never Land is a major one, as just described. For the infants, there may be a pirate ship, with fun-loving pirates, cake and ice cream, songs and lots of holding, which the infants love. This can cause them to choose to stay inside the internalized version of the pirate ship, and prevent their presenting (or healing).
It is difficult for littles to give up these internal representations, because they represent memories of fun, loving attention and joy in a life that had very little of these things. After a day of being tortured and programmed, the littles look forward to the fun setups such as Neverland.

There may be representations of the "Lost Boys" inside (beloved brothers and sisters), Wendy, Tinker Bell and other characters. Captain Hook is a powerful punisher inside, who punishes any disobedience to cult programming or attempts to leave Never Land. The goal of this internal world is to provide a place where these young parts live, and never come out – unless they are called out by programmers. In order to help these young parts to heal, they must be offered love and a life on the outside that is better than the virtual world created inside.

The internal carousels, circuses and other areas where younger parts live are all constructed by the programmers for a purpose: to reinforce cult directives, and keep internal reprogramming going with these younger parts. As the individual heals, and the littles step forward, they will have tremendous attachment needs and will want "playtime" with trusted adults.

Helping Littles Heal

In addition to love, younger parts will often want the following:

- Undivided adult attention
- Stories read to them
- Play time, whether playing with a hula hoop, going to a park and swinging, or coloring quietly. Different littles will have different needs, and will enjoy different activities. The main thing is that they will want to do them with **you**, the supporter, who they have come to trust.
- Most young parts have a good sense of humor, and enjoying teasing adults they trust. This is also part of healing, as they test out boundaries and discover what is okay and not in a normal relationship.
- Treats: the cult often heavily rewards littles who recontact with their favorite candy (such as chocolate) and tell them they are a "good girl" or "good boy". Littles like treats, and as the survivor heals, they may choose to give rewards to the younger parts for NOT contacting. It is better if treats chosen are different than those the cult uses, since the goal is to not reinforce programming.
- Bottles: the youngest (infant) parts may want a bottle. The survivor may choose to purchase a bottle and give the milk to the infants themselves, or choose a trusted, safe support person to give the bottle. Because giving bottles (and breast) is part of the bonding to programmers, the system may react with panic and anger if the infants begin to go to a "stranger" (non-cult person) for a bottle, since this means the programming is breaking down at a prime level. The infants themselves may react with fear if the internal parts are punishing them for accepting a bottle from an outsider, until the programming to only bond to programmers breaks. Other littles may only want the beloved trainer, and become angry at other parts who bond to a person outside the group. It is important that parts be allowed to express these conflicts, and receive acceptance, to help resolution of the conflicts.

Controllers and Communicators

Because cult children are genetically enhanced for intelligence, it is not unusual for even small infant parts to have at least some speech, and excellent understanding. But because the youngest infants inside may have trouble talking or being understood, there are often special parts known as communicators who communicate for these parts. The communicators for infants are often quite young, and programmed to be completely unemotional as they relay whatever the infants are experiencing. Communicators are often very compassionate and feel protective of the infants that they communicate for, and can become part of the "healing team" to help them heal.

Baby controllers are parts that oversee infant areas (see Pan above). There are other controllers, such as the internalized programmer(s) that the baby bonded to (often called "Papa" or "Mama" by the baby). This controller tells the infant what to do, and carries the baby past internal barriers without the baby getting punished. Once the controllers are willing to help with healing, there is less pain and punishment as the babies come forward to play and bond.

Why Littles Stay Young

Littles are young and stay young inside for several reasons. The primary reason they do so is that they were told to always stay young by their primary loved person (primary programmer) who has told them that they will not be loved if they grow older. As a result, the little makes a vow to the loved person to never grow up, to always stay young, and performs a ritual during which a demon is attached for this purpose. Once the demon leaves, and the vow is broken, and the little is able to come out and experience life, they will begin growing and developing, just as a normal child would (but more quickly). An infant does not take 18 years to "grow up" but instead may become a toddler and preschooler within months of coming out and interacting with a safe support person. This journey of growth is individual for each person. The love of the true (Christian) God is also very helpful in this growth, since the littles will feel safe with His presence nearby: they will feel safe enough to start breaking their programming, and grow up as they realize that God loves them.

Chapter 11: Reprogramming Systems

Reprogramming systems are systems designed to repair programs that begin breaking down, and keep systems and controllers doing their cult jobs. Reprogramming systems are actually specialized punishment systems, since they pull upon trauma to reinforce the programming. The main controllers in reprogramming systems will represent:

- A demonic deity (such as "Saturn", "Prometheus" or "Vulcan") with a familiar spirit attached to the human part. These parts run the reprogramming in different ways.
    - In general, there is a system that runs reprogramming 24 hours a day. This punishment is tied to triads of controllers: an infant, a child, and an older part, and each controller in each system will go through the reprogramming (pain) sequences. This system links to Epsilon (pain holding) system, in order to channel the pain and punishment for the reprogramming sequences.
    - Other systems will perform loyalty system reprogramming and punishments. This includes being pounded with "Vulcan's Hammer" and internal parts having their livers torn out by a large black bird as punishment for disobedience. This program is installed in infancy, when the programmers terrorize the infant with a large bird that claws them and is allowed to peck at them (they wear special goggles to protect the eyes).
    - Another system would punish the white systems and reprograms them in a manner similar to the prior system.
    - The birth mother (see chapter on "birth mother" for more on this controller)
- Other reprogramming controllers will include internalized trainers who are the primary trainers who have programmed the survivors. These trainers act in every way like the outside trainers, and will put the parts on training tables inside, and reprogram them as they were taught to do since early childhood.
- Other controllers include loved ones the survivor is bonded to (who may also be internalized trainers in dual roles). These loved ones are tortured, with screams, internally if the survivor's programming fails.

Most reprogramming systems run on a 24-hour cycle, with each system undergoing reprogramming during a two-hour time period for that day. Some systems work on a 48-hour cycle, but this is unusual. The reprogramming will work in the following manner:

1. The primary controllers for a system (such as the white Minerva or Athena for a presentation system) and the back command controllers (including deep delta for controllers) will communicate back and forth using specialized tones or "calls' that were installed in the womb and during infancy, and reinforced throughout life. These controllers are doing constant "system checks" with the controllers literally "singing" the tones back if the system is intact. If the system has been breached, or is no longer intact, the tone sung back (or its not being sung back) will represent this fact, and identify the problem (tones are used because information can be packed into each tone, and the brain processes these "calls" or "pings" between systems much more rapidly than conscious thought).

2. If a system call shows distress or faltering, or communicates that directives have been disobeyed, then the system will be reprogrammed. This can take place in several ways:

    a. For the presentations (white), the parts that have faltered or failed may be hospitalized in a re-enactment of the "Crazy Alice" scenes of torture, etc. in an internalized "hospital". The presentation parts will be escorted by doctors in white coats inside to "be made better" in the script, since any failure is considered being "sick" in the reprogramming script. Any failure of presenter amnesia (bleedthrough) will result in this, as well as any disobedience by presenters to cult commands.

    b. For more serious failures, internal parts may be taken to an internalized training facility that looks like the programming labs they are taken to for "tune ups" (reprogramming done to all cult members at intervals). This facility will be run inside by internalized representations of programmers who put the parts through an entire sequence of programming (shock, torture, tech torture, etc.) to get the part to continue doing its old job

    c. After the reprogramming, a complete system check is done again, to ensure that all parts are singing the correct tones back - and are in compliance.

If the reprogramming systems begin to fail, the parts controlling these systems are themselves tortured, and internal representations of loved ones are also tortured in an "if you fail, then ___ gets hurt" script.

Internal Demonic Activity

Without demonic interference or physical tune-ups, all programming would naturally fail over time. The human brain was not meant to forget, or to be controlled, or to do the things that occultic groups ask its members to do. The natural response is rebellion at the tremendous amount of emotional and physical time and energy required, and to question the motives for the horrendous abuse that cult groups engage in. To prevent this, cult groups rely heavily on demonic delusion to keep programming going.

This is why there are sacrifices and rituals performed before, during and after programming sessions. In addition, certain activities are programmed in to help ensure that the programming will not "fail". This includes:

- The installation of internal altars, and controllers performing sacrifices internally around the clock to maintain the internal demonic controls.
- Sexual activity with demons on the internalized altars, for greater control. All system controllers participate
- Spiritual (astral) contact in order to reprogram parts and influence the survivor to come back to the group, or to punish them for attempting to leave.
- In some groups, there are dimensions used for punishment purposes. If the survivor attempts to stop physical contact, their former handlers or programmers will attempt to astral in and drag them with them, where the demonic punishments cause great misery. This is why it is important to close all doors/portals for spiritual travel and access as quickly as possible.

Chapter 12: Suicidality and Self Harm

Suicide is an issue that comes up frequently for most survivors during the healing process. This is for several reasons:

- The survivor has learned over a lifetime to avoid painful or intense emotions in their presentations, and so has not learned to cope with them in a healthy way. Suicide may seem to be one way to "avoid the pain", and this thinking is aided by the demonic attachments.
- The demonization of parts: demons hate people, and want them dead. When a survivor is healing, and getting rid of the demonic, they realize that they are basically losing their "host". In retaliation, they will put thoughts of suicide in the survivor.
- Programming: most individuals programmed by sophisticated groups will have several layers of suicide/self-destruct in place, designed to "get rid of" the survivor should they become a security risk to the group.
- The survivor may be given a direct command by their group to die, especially if they are truly breaking free. This will be reinforced by the belief that their healing means that others they love are being tortured or killed. In many survivors, loyalty programming includes the willingness to die for the beloved programmers and loved ones in the group, and the desire to die rather than be a "traitor" is installed. This line of programming is activated when the survivor reaches the loyalty systems inside.

All survivors will have programming installed to believe that if they heal, and continue healing more deeply, they will die or suicide. This belief needs to be challenged, and truth brought to the parts that hold this.

A survivor who is doing intense healing work will need to openly discuss the possibility of suicide and what to do with suicidal feelings if they come up, with their therapist or support system. It is usually not a matter of "if" but "when" the feelings will come up, and a safety plan is critical. Talking about suicidal feelings will not "cause" the survivor to suicide, and can be a relief, since the feelings are there anyway.

Suicidal feelings can come at different intensity levels, ranging from a mild "I wish I could go to heaven and be free of all this pain" to an almost uncontrollable desire to self-harm. Any time the survivor shares they are feeling suicidal needs to be taken seriously, assessed, and the safety plan implemented (such as around the clock accountability and/or hospitalization) if the survivor feels they cannot control these impulses.

About Hospitalization

Some (but not all) survivors who are dealing with intense homicidal or suicidal feelings may need to go inpatient for a period of time to deal with the programming. If this is so, it is important to prayerfully consider where to go, since many hospitals have personnel that are mind controlled, and who will want to access the individual. In fact, there is programming installed in most survivors that makes them feel "I need to go to the hospital, I am sick" (part of the Crazy Alice programming sequence) in order to be re-accessed and reprogrammed.

There are some programs that are safer than others for inpatient hospitalization, but the survivor should be aware that even if the hospital itself is fairly safe, there may be other survivors inpatient who may attempt to access the survivor while they are inpatient. This is why in most cases, it is often best to provide around the clock prayerful support and accountability in preference to hospitalization, unless the crisis continues to escalate or becomes life-threatening. It is important to have input from a trained professional therapist if the risk of suicide is high.

Triggers for Suicide and Self Harm

As the survivor is healing, they will encounter various internal and external triggers for suicidality. Common triggers can include:

- **Breaching of a highly secure system inside**, by the survivor and/or therapist. These systems are often guarded by suicide programming, which can appear like "trip lines", "bombs", or simply guardians and controllers installed with suicide programming that runs with any unauthorized (i.e. someone other than the programmer) access

- **Beginning to bond with someone outside the group**: cult loyal parts will become extremely distressed as the survivor begins to make friends with and develop emotional attachments with individuals outside the cult group. This activates internal "anti-traitor" programming, in which the survivor throughout their life (in programmed scripts) has chosen to die rather than be a "traitor" (see traitor programming in the cult loyal programming chapter). They are dealing with the deep pain of being unable to see loved ones in the group, and may seek to wreak "revenge" on the parts choosing to leave the group by attempting to kill them through suicide. This intrasystem conflict and hostility needs to be processed and addressed openly, including allowing the cult loyal parts to process their own grieving without judgment (i.e. asking "How can you miss that S.O.B." will not help. Letting the survivor know that you see their pain and they are not alone in it will help more).

- **Subliminals**: these may come with commands and runes that order the survivor to die (in order to show their loyalty, or to have any hope of "ascension" etc.) When a survivor goes online, or uses a smart phone, they will be subjected to subliminals, and may feel suicidal or extremely depressed afterwards. Often, the subliminals will show loved ones in the cult group being tortured because of the survivor's unwillingness to obey cult commands. This is one reason why taking a break from going online, and minimizing any required online activity can be helpful, especially earlier in healing.

- **Seeing loved ones threatened**: if the survivor stops going to rituals or meeting with cult members, the group will eventually send people in public places to use hand signals to sign that they are being hurt and tortured, or will die soon. If the survivor works alone, or can be gotten alone, the loved one may raise their shirt, and show the bruises, cuts and welts from torture endured, with the survivor blamed. This type of interaction will cause intense suicidality, until the survivor has been able to recall who their double binds are, the messages they have been sending, how they are communicated, and then look at the traumas that caused them to take on a rescuer role for the loved one. The survivor will eventually need to come to the realization that it is not their fault if a loved one is hurt, abused or tortured, even if their leaving the group is blamed. The reality is that the loved one would be hurt anyway, as long as they remain in a group that abuses.

Anti-suicide Programming

Because suicidality can be so strong in individuals from organized groups, they may have undergone specific programming to stop or prevent suicide. They don't want to lose their best agents, but these agents may be dealing with painful traumas and emotions, causing the individual being programmed to give up. This may first be manifested as being a "failure to thrive" in infancy, which is very common in infants raised and programmed in facilities. Over 90% of all highly programmed infants go through at least one, and often several, episodes of failure to thrive (FTT) in which they stop eating, curl up and basically shut down.

The remedy used by programmers is to stop the programming, and let the infant spend bonding time with the programmers and other infants, such as their twins. These other infants can often pull the infant back from death, and help the infant want to live again.

As the individual gets older, specific programming to not self harm and not commit suicide is put in, with heavy rewards and praise for wanting to stay alive.

During especially difficult times (such as the time after attempting to carry a nephilim baby, or the time after a marriage to a principality at age 13, or completing the full rites of initiation into adulthood at age 12 – 13 when numerous sacrifices are done) the individual may again fall into a "spiritual coma" and want to die – and again, is brought out of it by the loving bonding with the people they are closest to. These individuals gather around the spiritually wounded person, and attempt to help restore the desire to live. If unsuccessful, the individual will die; if successful, they will continue living.

The individual will also be programmed with codes to prevent them from committing suicide, with command codes designed to stop them from suicide. These commands will be given in times of the individual feeling deeply suicidal, in order to keep them alive (if they are still active in the group).

Emotions that Can Precipitate Self Harm

During healing, when various emotions come up, certain ones can precipitate suicidal feelings and self-harm more than others. Despair, rage, rejection and feeling abandoned are the primary ones. These are all extremely painful emotions, and the survivor may feel completely overwhelmed and incapable of dealing with them. Healing can include looking at the traumas that caused the feelings, and helping the parts work through the feelings with safe support. The survivor needs to know that suicide is a permanent "non-solution" to a temporary problem: intense feelings. It can help if they come to realize that they will not always feel this way, and that most feelings subside within a matter of days, including the most painful emotions.

Unsafe Behaviors/Risk Taking

When an individual is attempting to avoid feeling emotional pain, they may cope by exhibiting unsafe behaviors. They may go out late at night alone, trawl bars, engage in unsafe sex, or go through multiple relationships quickly with relative strangers. Other behaviors can include driving rapidly on curving roads, or taking other risks with their life.

Some behaviors can be caused by addictions, such as sexual addictions designed to keep the individual hooked to the group. Other causes can be an unconscious desire to suicide, or to re-enact experiences of abuse due to guilt.

Chapter 13: Working with the Birth Mother

In most systems programmed with modern methods, birth mother trauma is a basic foundation for the programming. The internal birth mother is a prime programmed part, and will hold within her all programming scripts, put in with birth mother trauma.

What is birth mother trauma? While the methods will vary some, it involves incredible cruelty to the birth mother carrying the fetus, in order to increase the susceptibility to control.

Not every occultic group does this to their infants. But many groups, especially international groups, will do this in their programming labs. The zygotes are first created in petri dishes, with genetically enhanced material. The birth mothers are then taken to the programming labs, where they are told that they were "specially selected" to "carry a very special baby." These are healthy, fit young women (ages 18 to 26, on average), who may have been bred for this purpose: to be an incubator for a genetically enhanced fetus. The birth mothers are excited, and shown the "joys" of having a wonderful baby by actors who pretend to be birth mothers who recently had their babies, and hold up the smiling, happy infants. They discuss how wonderful it is to be a birth mother, in order to set up the later betrayal.

The excited mother is implanted with the zygote, and for several days is treated like royalty: the best foods, wonderful treatment, the chance to stroll in a nearby garden, and to chat with the other expectant mothers. But within a week, the trauma begins. The birth mother will be strapped in a chair, and one of her digits (finger joint) cut off, because she "disobeyed." Over the next few weeks, the birth mother's life becomes a nightmare, as she is put through the following scenarios:

- Commanded to obey an order, such as to pick up a block, color in a circle, or other commands. Instant obedience is rewarded. She is then given a command that is impossible to obey (such as to climb a high wall beyond her ability), and with the infraction, is tortured, while the programmers tell her and the developing fetus, "disobedience brings pain, while obedience brings joy."
- She is chained to a wall, and sleep deprived.
- She is brutally raped by people, by animals, by a false "jesus" as programming scripts for the fetus are played out.
- By the end of the sixth month, her toes, feet, fingers and hands will have been chopped off, as well as her nose, for "disobediences". She is forced to eat food from a dog dish on the floor, and is treated terribly.
- By the end of the seventh month, she is almost unrecognizable as a human being, with

her hair having been pulled out, numerous skinnings, her teeth pulled out, numerous rapes, being sent to "hell" for "punishment" (to install this in the fetus), her nose and ears chopped off, and basically only the torso is left. At this point, the birth mother's mind will have also gone, and she will be in a nearly catatonic state from the despair and torture.

At this point, the fetus's primary programmers will step in, talking to the fetus, telling it things like "I love you" "I can't wait for you to be born", and other scripts to encourage bonding to these trainers. The fetus is experiencing the terror of abandonment by the birth mother in the womb (due to her trauma response), has already experienced numerous rejection traumas (the birth mother being told that the fetus is responsible for her pain as she is tortured, and her then screaming "get it out", "I hate you" or even attempting to beat her womb); this primes the fetus to bond extremely heavily to the primary programmers in the womb to escape the despair of rejection and abandonment.

It may seem incredible that the birth mother does not abort the embryo/fetus with the enormous amount of trauma, but the programming facilities use state-of-the-art technology (at least 50-75 years more advanced than that publicly known), to carefully monitor the vital signs of both the mother and fetus; and to administer medications that prevent contractions and aborting of the fetus.

Fetal Response to Birth Mother Traumas (Love/Hate)

In the traumas described above, the fetus will feel a deep split in the core between love for the birth mother (on whose life the fetus depends, a God-given and natural response for the one who carries the baby), and growing rage and hate towards her due to the rejections. This will cause a primary split in the fetus between parts that love the birth mother ("good babies" labeled so by the programmers and the fetus itself) and those who hate her and want to destroy her ("bad babies" labeled so by the fetus's guilt at feeling this way).

This creates the primary split along which the white and black systems will be created. The fetus cannot deal with and reconcile the emotional overwhelm of its mother being traumatized, and basically programmed to hate the fetus over the course of the pregnancy. This maternal rejection then creates the base foundation for the fetus bonding to the programmers (in desperation to survive emotionally) and being controlled by them.

Internally, the fetus will have created representations of the birth mother. One is the "fantasy mother" that is loving and nurturing, and asks the fetus to forgive it for rejecting it (this is overlaid with VRs over the years) and represents a "good birth mother" to the fetus. The other is a punishing, vengeful, rejecting birth mother who wants to destroy the fetus. This creates the base for omega and other self-destruct programming, since it ties to the core and core splits as a primary trauma.

Finally, the birth mother will be internalized by the fetus (with demonic help) as a victim or torture and brutality, that needs to be "rescued" by the fetus (in a manner similar to setups in which the fetus is told that the birth mother will be "punished less" if the fetus will agree to take some of the pain; the fetus does, and is shocked or hurt, then praised for doing so. This is the base for epsilon, or pain-holding programming.

The template for every major program is installed in the womb in the developing fetus. Because the fetus has no contact with external reality other than the words the programmers use during scripts, there is little "reality check" to the programming sequences, and the fetus will hold the programming using the "magical thinking" that infants often use. There does not have to be any connection to reality in the programming installed prenatally, since there is no external reality to contradict it. This is the goal; to embed lies in the subconscious before the infant is ever born, and to construct a whole paradigm of belief regarding the world during this time.

Birth Trauma and Delusion

Once the infant is born, the birth mother is immediately killed. The infant is then told "you killed her." Because of the fetal rage at rejection by the birth mother, and the desire to destroy her (enhanced by demons the fetus accepts), the infant believes this lie; after all, part of the infant *did* want her to die.

The internal birth mother is kept intact, as a core controller. This is one of the first delusions: the belief that the birth mother never died, which resolves the subconscious pain and guilt and trauma related to the birth death. This delusion is kept intact using VRs of the birth mother (who was filmed throughout the pregnancy), who alternates being loving and nurturing; or accusing and angry. If the infant obeys the programmers, the birth mother is "happy" and is "not punished" inside; if the infant disobeys, she becomes angry and punishing internally.

When the survivor attempts to leave the cult group, and heal, the group will first attempt to trigger this programming with subliminals of an angry birth mother, or of a birth mother destroying her fetus (causing the internal birth mother to "turn" on the internal fetal parts and attempt to destroy them, in omega programming).

If this does not work, then the group will often find a "body double" of the birth mother, and use this individual to attempt to access the survivor. Due to the unhealed prenatal traumas, the survivor may be susceptible to this access until they have consciously resolved the internal emotional pain, guilt and rage, and the deep abandonment wounds caused by the rejection in the womb.

Birth mother programming is a core level program. While the birth mother internally is not the core, she will sit next to the core, "protecting" her from the realization that the real birth mother is dead (the core does not realize this, due to delusion and the demonic). To heal this level of trauma requires loving, prayerful support, and the chance for the survivor to process the painful emotions associated with the prenatal traumas.

Only the Christian (true) God can heal this level of trauma, which is why prayer, fasting (if there are no medical contraindications) and nurturing support are needed for healing. Fetal parts may come out literally thrashing in anger and pain about their traumas and rejection, and may need to know that they are loveable and loved. Fetuses often "hum" with rage or intense emotions internally, and may come out humming or making other preverbal noises. At first, they may not be able to communicate directly, but will need to communicate through a communicator part.

The internal birth mother will be extremely wounded, extremely demonized (as the fetal parts are, too), and will need love, support and prayer. Over time, as she comes to faith in the real Jesus, she can heal. She will need to process her own feelings of rage towards the programmers, towards God (who she was taught to blame, since He didn't stop the abuse), and the fetal parts inside (who hurt her in VRs designed to increase the system hostility and splits between the birth mother and the fetuses.

Love heals and these parts will need the modeling of what real love looks like, since they have never experienced it themselves. If they are to want to know the Christian God, they will need a safe person who can communicate what His love is like, not in words, but in actions. Gentle grounding, spending time talking and listening to the parts, and other demonstrations of love will mean much more than "Christian lectures" or a gospel presentation. These parts will be quick to embrace Christianity once they experience real Christian love; otherwise, they will stay hidden inside – and make the survivor vulnerable to access.

Core level work cannot be done without loving support. The survivor was hurt horrendously in the womb, and cannot simply fix "themselves" (how they wish they could!). This is a tough journey to help someone with, but is well worth it as the survivor and the core parts begin to "get it" and really heal.

Chapter 14: Working with the Core

Most people who enter therapy for ritual abuse and mind control are looking for relief from their pain: the emotional, physical and spiritual pain that has driven their life since before conscious memory. They may wonder why "it's taking so long" or why they often must battle to undo programming. Finally, near the end of the journey, it starts to all make sense, when they meet the core and the core system.

This is where the most deeply guarded secrets, beliefs and loves are kept. The survivor who "really wants to know" their entire life history, will find this area deeply guarded – because they **wanted** to hide from themselves this knowledge. For an occultic system, the deepest love (yes, love) and loyalty to Satan and his son (the "antichrist" but called "he who has come", "the light of the world" and other names by these groups) resides. The survivor will find at core level the conflicts that have driven the rest of the system, and impeded healing.

This realization can feel overwhelming, unless there is adequate support in place. To learn how truly dedicated one has been to evil, and the amount of rage and pain the survivor holds towards God and the universe is difficult, to put it mildly. On top of this is the guilt as the survivor not only hears about, but knows and recalls what she/he did to others in that state of pain, over the years as a cult member. The individual doing core work needs a supportive other, including God and prayerful friends, to help pull them through this part of the journey, because the emotions are deep.

Core Trauma and Bonding

The core is the primary controller for the other systems, even if the programming is "non-hierarchical" inside. This young (often aged two) part will run the show, but is kept very young and extremely bonded to Satan. This is accomplished through numerous setups, with a classic one (developed by Mengele) in which the birth mother and fetus are tortured together. The birth mother is told to "pray to God" for help and to make the torture stop. Both she and the fetus scream out to God together – and the pain is made worse.

This creates a tremendous amount of rage towards God in the fetus, who cannot understand why God seemingly did not answer this scream for help in the womb. In response, the fetus turns in anger away from God, and a demonic spirit (Satan or another spirit) enters into the heart of the fetus, promising to allow the fetus to grow big, powerful, and one day get revenge on God and mankind (who the core now hates because of the pain they have endured at the hands of human beings).

This, or a similar setup, is done in which the fetus chooses to turn away from the true God, and sets themselves up (with demonic "protection") as their own "rescuer" from the pain –

and is the basis for all later programming to hate God and men (including themselves), which lies in the core system. **All core programming in international occultic groups will cause the fetus to turn away from God, hate Him, and choose to rescue itself, with the help of the demonic**. This opens the doorway for demonic bonding (the real goal of core trauma and programming) during which the demonic promises the core that it will "take away the pain" if allowed in. The fetus agrees, and dissociation, deception and delusion enter in, including false beliefs about God (the demonic portrays Him as hateful and uncaring), and about the self (the fetus believes that it can "rescue" others by taking their pain, or becoming powerful through allowing demons in). The fetus will be strongly bonded to the demonic, and in many groups, the core and core system surrounding it will only be allowed to interact with demons, and not with human beings.

When the infant is born, and the core (and its system) are out, actors dressed as "demons" and "spiritual beings" with crystal eyes in the masks (to prevent bonding with the human) feed, care for, rock and bond with these parts of the infant. They will sing songs, and tell the infant core that they love her/him. As the infant gets bigger, and develops spiritual abilities, the actors are no longer needed, since the demonic will take the bonding memories the infant has, and begin doing the bonding activities. The infant will actually be lifted up and rocked by the demonic, and the core will believe that Satan (or another spirit) is the only being that truly loves him/her – or has ever loved him/her. The core will have a deep hatred of all humans, which is reinforced with numerous setups.

Anti-Mortal Programming

The fetus in the womb will be told that they are an "immortal spirit" that has been "trapped" in a human, or mortal body, by a cruel God who wanted them to feel the "pain of mortality". The fetus in most groups will have been put through a "seal of mortality" programming session, in which the womb is injected with a drug that causes incredible fetal pain (searing throughout), and both the fetus and mother scream in pain, while the programmers tell the fetus that they are experiencing "the pain of the mortal seal" that "seals" them into a mortal body.

The fetus vows to never re-experience this terrible emotional and physical pain and terror. A demon offers to "take the pain away" and the fetus agrees – giving the pain "away" to the demon, and dissociating from the physical body.

Due to this and other experiences (pain and trauma to the physical body) the fetus and later infant core and systems come to absolutely hate and loathe their "mortal" (lower, descended) body, and will attempt to dissociate. This creates a barrier between the core and lower systems, which the core views as "mortal" and requiring "ascension."

Because the core is programmed to stay inside (unless called out by "Satan") and to never interact with humans, there is very little real world experience to degrade the programming and beliefs of the core. Instead, the core is counseled by demons, and will often live inside within an internal Garden of Eden or similar structure, completely insulated from daily life, which the other parts live.

Yet the core will be quite aware if parts attempt to break their programming (which is viewed as unacceptable "descending") and will immediately call upon system controllers to punish parts attempting to heal.

Hatred of Mortals Programming

In most organized groups, the core will be programmed, along with the core system, to hate all mankind (hate all "mortals"). Satan (or a similar spirit) will pet her, woo her and tell her that she and he will live when all others are gone, soothing the core's terrible fear of abandonment. It is not unusual for the core to have a deep friendship with the demonic, which comes nightly to visit, provides counsel, and promises to "love her always". The core stays young (around age two or so) to please Satan, who has told her that he will not love her any more if she grows older.

The core will have absolutely no memory of the terrible abuse that this spirit exacts from other ("lower") systems, or will not care if she hears, since in her reality, it is "me and Satan" and the rest of the world does not matter.

The core will be programmed to absolutely hate mortal men, with setups in which during prenatal development, "mortals" come and torture her and the birth mother, laughing and raping, etc. As an infant, when the core is out, setups are done in which "mortals" give the infant bottles that cause searing pain and nausea; burn the infant, rape her, torture her, skin her, and tell her "this is what mortals like to do." They will pretend to attempt to "eat" the infant alive, causing great terror, until she is "rescued" by Satan in the setup.

After dozens of experiences like this, the infant core will scream if a human comes near, and calm down only when Satan comes and comforts him or her.

When a survivor is healing, and begins doing core work, it can help to realize that the supporters the survivor is working with may be the first human beings that he or she has ever interacted with (other than during a brief traumatic setup) in her life. The amount of fear and terror that may come forward can be intense; the core may have never seen human eyes looking at her kindly, and must work through this initial terror.

The core will be reluctant to come out, and with good reason. All of her interactions with human beings prior to this point have been intensely traumatic, and she must have time to "test the waters" and ensure that the outside support is safe. She is also deeply bonded to Satan, and will have intense grief and self-hatred at the thought of losing this love object if the survivor continues to heal. The anger and grief will often fuel internal self-punishment to prevent healing, until the core is able to receive enough information from the real world to choose to give up Satan and to allow others to care for her.

Core Controllers and Guardians

Around the core will be splits that are equally bonded to the demonic and with equal hatred of humans (or "mortals"). It is common for several initial splits to occur: the 4 princes of hell and the 7 generals of hell; along with 24 "elders". These surround the internal "Satan" who sits on a "throne" (note: this is also represented in other systems beneath the core system), and these represent core guardians/protectors. Their job is to ensure that the core and the internal Satan (punishing aspect) never fail; while the core bonds to Theo (the loving, "caring" aspect of Satan).

These parts inside have demonic attachments, and constantly perform sacrifices, offer hymns of praise, and stand guard to protect the core from outside influences; they also have sex with outside demons and the core to reinforce programming. The demonic sexual activity and rituals "recharges" the internal programs, and occurs daily.

As the survivor gets in touch with the memories, and the life history (which involves breaking agreements by the core to never share information with other systems and parts; and the parts and systems breaking those same agreements to never hear information from the core and the core system, including repentance from the rites, rituals, covenants, vows to demons and to trainers to never remember these things), emotions will start coming up. The survivor will have already dealt with a significant amount of anger, pain, guilt and terror over the years while doing healing work; but the core layer of these feelings can seem particularly intense due to the fact that the emotions are held by fetal parts attached to the core controllers and parts, and the core.

The deepest layers of rage (including feeling homicidal), despair (and feeling suicidal) and guilt (feeling completely cut off from any hope of God's forgiveness) as well as the feelings of rage against God will come up. Because this conflicts with the survivor's Christianity, these feelings can cause deep discomfort as they come forward; but they must be dealt with, since they have fueled the survivor's base programming their entire life. They are simply out in the open now, and do not surprise God (although their depth and intensity may surprise both the survivor and their supporter(s)).

Core despair can be difficult, and trigger extreme depression and suicidality. The despair of realizing that the core was "tricked' by Satan and the other demons, and that the whole life was built upon lies, can be devastating. This is not something that the person can work out with logic (i.e. "I shouldn't feel this way, because…" or "of course Satan tricks people, he's a liar").

While these things are true, the core and these parts need comfort, and healing attachments to overcome the betrayals and lies of a lifetime.

The core will also battle some extreme delusions as well that will impede healing until resolved. Even though the birth mother is usually killed at birth, the core will not realize or believe this, because there is an internal representation of the birth mother. This is very difficult for the core and the prime splits to deal with, and can cause tremendous pain and grieving. The fetal parts will want to deny that she is dead, and it takes time for these parts to realize the truth.

The primary core terror is abandonment. This is triggered in the fetus by the birth mother losing her mind due to the months of torture she underwent; when her mind goes and withdraws from the fetus, the fetus feels incredible terror. To deal with the terror, the fetus agrees to accept a demon that represents the birth mother; this is a prime dissociation that keeps the whole dissociative reality going inside (see the chapter on the "birth mother" for more information).

Working with the core requires helping the survivor work through this terror of being all alone in the world. This can be accomplished by:

- Praying with (and for) the survivor and helping the core and core splits realize how much the Christian (true) God loves them. This is the primary source of healing, since the original wound was turning away in rage and pain from God and His love. Once the core becomes a Christian, the system can began making better choices. But realize that the core will need discipleship: like any abused child, the core will not at first understand how Christians act, or why talking with demons is unsafe. Patience and role modeling love can help tremendously.

- Loving the survivor, with nurturing, sitting quietly with them in their grief; letting them vent their pain and rage, and not judging them for the process or feelings they are having. Synchronizing with another's pain, especially at this level, can be difficult, and supporters and the survivor will need to build in breaks and joy building to help offset the tremendously draining emotional work required

- Working on building real life, good experiences for the core and the core system, especially with human beings. Whether having a good cup of coffee with core controllers and enjoying a beautiful morning; or holding the hand of a young part that has only experienced torture from humans and showing them that not all humans hurt, this kind of new information will help the whole system heal.

Chapter 15: Building Joy

In order to heal, the survivor cannot simply do trauma work and not have times of experiencing refreshment or joy. Attempting to do a lot of inside work without breaks and joy building will cause burnout, because the survivor will simply not have any "good life" to heal towards. They will become good at "healing" but not at relating to others, or self nurture, and so will bring emotionally unhealed parts together – and continue to distance from caring support. They will also be unable to nurture others in their healing journey, if they have not themselves received safe support and seen caring modeled for them.

So, how does a person working on intense emotions and dealing with terrible trauma build joy, when simply getting out of bed in the morning may seem like a major achievement? Or when depression that feels completely overwhelming hits? This is when the person may need to pace the joy building, and use whatever tools work for them in that moment.

Receiving a hug can build joy on the hardest days. Sharing a prayer request, and seeing the caring in another's eyes can build joy.

Soaking in prayer, and spending time in worship (which is a true "sacrifice of praise" on the hardest days) can build joy and hope. God's love never fails, and He can provide the hope that keeps the individual going on the worst days, when the demonic tries to whisper "you'll never heal, you'll always feel this way." This is a lie, and the victory comes not just from commanding the demonic to leave, but then experiencing the love of God, His comfort, and His reassurances that healing is possible –and is happening. The survivor may need to hear these truths frequently from supporters as well, even daily. The worship time can include listening to uplifting music, and even dance. One of the most meaningful moments in my healing journey came during a time when I was mourning the loss of my husband and adult children, due to my choice to stop all contact since they were all still cult active. As I lay on my bed crying, I put on a worship CD, and began through my tears to worship the LORD, who I knew does love me. I stood to dance. At that moment, I felt the true Jesus at my side, asking "May I have this dance?" He held me in His arms, and we danced together, and I experienced His wonderful love. I have never forgotten this experience and the hope and encouragement it brought me.

Music is especially healing because it ministers to the right brain, where feelings are stored. It can enter in, and bring truth into the emotional parts of the brain, which is why it is important to carefully guard the type of music (or any entertainment) listened to.

Fun activities, such as going to a park, walking on a beach, gardening, flying a kite, playing with a pet, or telling silly jokes are also joy building. Some people enjoy painting and writing, but this should be balanced with "together time" with other people, since having fun is even more so with a friend. Hiking is good for both the body and emotions, as are boating, swimming and other physical activities. One fun activity is rolling down a hill of grass (check for rocks, sticks or doggie deposits first!), or rolling on the floor and humming (an exercise used for brain healing) which usually causes lots of giggling in those who do it. Make a list of the things you really enjoy doing, both quiet and active, and have it available to consider on days when you need to build joy and take a break.

About TV

It can be easy to simply want to vegetate in front of the TV on emotionally tough days, but this should not be your primary relaxation for several reasons. Vegetating is not physically healthy, and being sedentary can increase depression. In addition, TV feeds subliminals constantly, reinforcing programming to welcome Alexis (the calm voice that will help with crowd control) and the New World Order (in fact, the subliminals are part of Project Alexis, or the mind control techniques being used to prepare the general population for the advent of their occultic ruler). All videos, CDs, computer games and other digital media now have subliminals embedded, that are fed at 0.03 microseconds. They are undetectable with ordinary equipment (you can't "stop the video and see the subliminal, because the images will be blurred and fade into the background, and are only visible when the media is moving). The equipment required to view these subliminals costs hundreds of thousands of dollars, which most people do not own.

Pray about your TV viewing, and about how much is appropriate. It can make a real difference in how you feel, whether you are a survivor or not. It is amazing how desensitized our population has become to sex, violence and the occult due to this mind control technology that sits in everyone's living room.

Spending time being nurtured, and nurturing others is joy building. Letting a friend give you a hug, getting a foot rub, or other physical touch (that is nonsexual, with a safe person) is very healing. If you know a Christian massage therapist and can afford it, this is a good way to have safe touch, which is healing. Be aware that any physical contact, no matter how safe, can bring up powerful emotions due to the abuse; this is a chance to work on these issues and feelings.

Taking care of a pet, or helping care for a friend's child, or other ways of giving can also be joy building. Pets love unconditionally, and do require love, attention and care. Be prayerful, and be in a place financially and emotionally to take on this care before getting one.

Praying for others can be joy building. As you minister to others, and intercede, you also experience healing.

Volunteering (at a <u>safe</u> place) is joy building and can help build your personal gifts in a new setting. While your life may have revolved around "doing" for the cult, with talents and skills hijacked by the demonic, this is now a chance to use your abilities, surrendered to God, to help others. Most people who have survived programming by an organized group will have wonderful talents, but may feel ashamed of them. They may wonder, "What kind of life can an ex-assassin have?" or "How can a former cult programmer have a good life in the day-to-day world?" or "What does a former cult geneticist do?" These are understandable questions, but each person will have abilities and talents used in doing those jobs, that can be used to help others once the memories and traumas are worked through. A person may be physically strong who had lots of military training, and so can help cut trees and grass, shovel snow and do repairs for an elderly person.

A person who is highly organized can use this skill to help in a ministry office, or help clean houses for others. A person who enjoys plants can grow a garden, and share the produce with others in need. A person with a background in behavioral sciences can use the skills of being a good listener to help others. This is why it is important to pray, and ask God to show you what your true talents and gifts are, and how to start using them when the time is right.

Giving to others is one of the most joy-building activities possible. It helps to bring meaning to the person coming out of a life of pain, and helps the individual to see that they have real value outside of the group. One caution: it is important to not get into a "works" mentality, which is common when first leaving a group that literally works its members to exhaustion. It is okay to allow yourself a season of rest as you heal, and then to very gradually begin giving. At first, giving may simply be tithing to your church, until there is enough healing to give in other, nonfinancial ways.

Being with Others

It is difficult to heal alone. I have known survivors who attempted to do most of the healing journey "solo" and in most cases, they were either accessed (because the loneliness pulled cult loyal parts back), or they integrated, but never healed relationally. They accomplished the goal of staying away from the cult, but were walking wounded since they never received the nurture and support needed for full emotional health after doing the internal work.

Some survivors may have no other choice, since there is simply no safe support where they live, and they are unable to leave due to finances. There is also a severe shortage of safe houses (the only one I was in was the house of a friend from church, who was the only non-cult friend I had; she kindly allowed me to stay with her during part of my healing journey). I personally do not know of any "safe houses" that are publicly known, and neither do most of the churches and ministries I have contacted over the years.

This is why building safe support is a prayerful journey. Who do your parts tell you is safe? They will know who is unsafe, and you should listen to them. If you feel uneasy around someone, ask inside why. If you feel deep rage towards someone, and have no conscious idea of why, ask inside parts.

Building support might involve asking yourself about Bible Study or church members, who to approach, and how, and how much to share. You should be very cautious if you feel an "instant connection" with someone, since this is often programmed in; you will likely feel most comfortable with people from a similar background as yours, so it is important to check inside regarding what types of interactions you are having, and whether there are any "red flags" that parts see.

In general, you should be the one to approach people for support, and not the other way around. In my personal healing journey, every time someone approached me offering to "help" it was a setup. The safe people I found were because I developed friendships slowly, over time (as in several years), parts watched and evaluated the interactions I had, and decided that they were probably okay.

There are numerous people programmed to be therapists and to offer support to survivors, who are actually mind controlled and unaware. This is why the survivor needs to be cautious when approaching others for support. I have personally seen or lived the following situations:

- A caring survivor who offered to be friends and support (they were cult active)
- A husband who drove me to therapy, was very supportive of healing, and wanted to do "everything possible to help her heal" (he was my handler)
- Ministries that supposedly help survivors that were actually sexually abusing people and verbally berating them
- The offer to stay in a house from a survivor, recommended to me by a large church, who ended up accessing me
- Four therapists who were survivors of mind control (including two who disclosed their own memories of severe abuse and losing time to me, and said "This is normal, don't worry if it happens," and another who kept saying "I feel like I'm going down a rabbit hole" when I shared memories with her. I stopped seeing them).

There are also safe people and ministries out there, and it is important to carefully pray, ask God for wisdom and discernment, before you approach them for support.

Most large churches are infiltrated – but this does not negate the good, sincere, non-cult members of the church who can be good support. Many small churches are also infiltrated as well, so it takes prayer and discernment to know who to reach out to. Prayer ministry at a church can be wonderful, but again, be careful who you allow to "lay hands" on you. I have a somewhat humorous (now) story regarding this. I went for several months to stay in an area where a large mega-church ministry is located, with lots of revival. I wanted healing, and a closer walk with God.

I went with a safe support person to look for housing. The house I had originally arranged to live in did not work out, so my supporter and I prayed for a roommate. Suddenly, a woman sitting next to us said, "Oh, do you need a place to live? I am looking for a roommate". It seemed like a "miracle", an answer to prayer. My supporter and I had dinner with her, I felt oh, so comfortable with the woman right away. She was a minister's wife (he had passed away) and she was in fulltime ministry. But I also started to feel extremely uneasy, especially as her story unfolded; her father had committed suicide, and she herself had some unusual emotional issues. I told my supporter that I believed this woman was unsafe, especially when I learned that she and the other woman who would be living there called another woman who was to room with them, telling her that she couldn't. In other words, the "we need a roommate" was a manufactured story! My supporter did not believe me and left town. The minute she left, the roommates began accessing and threatening me.

I fled the house and went into a women's shelter for safety. The next weekend, I saw my former "roommate" in a prayer walk; she immediately came walking towards me, saying, "I want to lay hands on you and impart the Spirit to you!" I began walking away, faster and faster, until she was almost literally running after me. I left the room, and sat next to two people I knew, saying, "I don't want her to come near me."

This is an example of situations that can occur, when those in "ministry" are still unhealed and unaware. I did disclose to church leadership about the situation (which is biblical), and chose to leave that area of the country. I did later find true safe support in another state.

Chapter 16: Relating to Support People

For many survivors, it is difficult to build supportive relationships, and relate to people outside of the cult group they were born into. This is true for various reasons. For instance, most survivors of modern mind control by international groups were born into facilities, heavily programmed in the womb and throughout childhood, lived in a barracks-type setting with their age mates (whom they consider brothers and sisters), and bonded to trainers as their primary parental figures. They were allowed to live in families in various nations for only a few weeks a year (and in the past ten years, according to some survivor reports, in some facilities, there is NO presentation programming at all; the presentation itself is completely loyal to the New World Order and their Leader).

Imagine someone raised like this leaving a group, and attempting to live in a "normal" family setting. Instead of going on missions (to assassinate someone), or working in a programming facility or genetics lab, or overseeing the human trafficking trade in a third world nation, which has been 90 percent of their reality prior to leaving the group, the survivor is now asked to go to Bible Studies, smile and "act Christian" in a world that has almost no comprehension of what they have been through (and often makes evident they have no desire to learn about).

It is difficult, to say the least. The skills needed to run missions or labs are very different from those needed to make – and keep – long-lasting, supportive friendships. Issues come up, and the survivor must attempt to learn to live in a society that is as unfamiliar to them as possible. The survivor will be used to eating in group settings or military camps; with others who make coarse jokes and survive the harsh reality with dark humor and bitter cynicism.

While many survivors can be "charming" while on missions, deep down they are not really "warm and fuzzy" people that churches and supporters naturally are drawn to. They are tough, even bitter realists, and are clearly aware of the evil side of humanity. Yet, they are also deeply loyal to and loving of those few individuals they come to trust.

Common Issues with Support Relationships

Many times, those who support survivors of mind control will have problems understanding the survivor, since the world they were raised in is literally so different than normal society. The support person will want to understand, but the relatively insulated world of most support people will not have prepared them adequately for confronting the reality of the evil and brutality that most individuals coming out of mind controlled groups have survived.

It is very common for supporters to wonder why it is "taking so long" for the survivor to heal, and many have very unrealistic expectations of healing. Healing from a lifetime of sophisticated mind control will usually take years (as in five, six, seven or more) to heal; if the survivor is accessed, then the time required for healing increases.

There are no "quick fixes" for survivor issues; but many ministries and supporters want to "hurry along" the process before the survivor is ready. This does survivors a disservice; and those who choose to minister to survivors should be prepared to count the cost, and to be there for the "long haul". It is extremely damaging to abandon survivors in the midst of their healing; this is literally their "worst fear" realized. If you become unable to continue providing support, you should have backup people in place, who can step in and offer the help needed in a crisis.

Survivors will often sabotage their support relationships (see chapter on "Working With Cult Loyal Parts" for more information). They may become hostile, angry and forget to thank you for helping them break free of the cult during the time they are in intense pain and their systems are punishing the crud out of them for trying to leave. The survivor may become extremely irritable, will argue with you, or do everything possible to test the relationship, because they have never been allowed to be honest with someone before in their life and not be abused.

These behaviors are actually a sign that the survivor is beginning to trust the supporter, and the cult loyal and hostile parts are coming out, and "checking things out." But many supporters do not recognize this fact, or are emotionally immature themselves, and may respond back with anger, belittling or abandonment. They may attempt to "preach at" the survivor, instead of loving them. The supporter may ask emotionally devastating questions such as "Where is your faith? Why aren't you healing yet?" when the survivor is trying their best to heal as quickly as possible.

There may be a push for a mass deliverance and "quick integration" in someone who is still early in their healing journey. This will backfire, since the survivor deep down will know that they have not resolved their issues with God, man, or themselves yet, and may feel despair at their inability to "perform" in a Christian manner.

No one pressures the survivor to heal more than the survivor themselves. They need support, not criticism or misunderstanding in the process of healing.

Preventing Support Burnout

Support burnout is an issue for those who help survivors of ritual abuse and mind control. Support means walking with people who are deeply traumatized; operate at a very young level of maturity initially, and who require nurturing and understanding. They also need strong accountability until their systems are inaccessible. These needs can cause burnout in supporters, who may resent the time and effort that helping a survivor requires.

The ideal is for the survivor to have a safe support team that can take turns helping the survivor, which includes a therapist skilled in working with mind control and abuse issues. In reality, this ideal does not exist. The survivor will have to work hard at developing multiple areas of support, to prevent burning out the people who are helping them in their journey.

Avoiding the "Scary" Label

Many churches are frightened about helping survivors of ritual abuse or mind control. The media has done a pretty thorough job of portraying mind control survivors as borderline sociopaths; killers; or crazy people seeking attention, none of which are true. Movies depict the demonic as scary and powerful, with graphic scenes of attacks on "Christians" which have nothing to do with our real authority in Christ. I have literally had Satan appear in the room, and he had to leave quietly with a simple command in Jesus's name; he has no authority at all when a believer stops giving it to him (out of fear or ignorance).

The survivor needs to learn how and when to disclose to their church about their background. In some cases, the right answer may be "never" since many churches are completely untaught regarding how to help survivors. In most cases, the best choice is "slowly". I have seen survivors walk into churches and at the first service they have visited, gone forward to the prayer team and pastors (who are strangers) and announce they are survivors of ritual abuse. In most cases, this does not allow the chance to develop relationship, and instead, the survivor gets labeled negatively from the start.

This can be a form of self sabotage. It is much better to get to know the church and members, participate in Bible studies, and over time slowly share small portions of your background, such as sexual abuse. See how folks react to that. Over time, as they get to know you as a real person, who is willing to pray for them and give back, they may be more able to hear more about your past. In most churches, you the survivor will be the first teacher they have regarding ritual abuse and mind control, and it can be positive if you take time to develop relationships with those you teach.

Those who support survivors will often deal with cult threats, either directly (phone calls, etc.) or indirectly (warfare, messages relayed by the survivor). In most cases, these threats are not acted upon, for a reason: churches and supporters with a strong faith in God will have significant protection. I have heard from numerous cult members who shared that they were unable to kill someone, or fulfill a mission to sabotage a ministry, due to the strong angelic protection that blocked them.

When threats come, give them to God, who can handle it. He is bigger and more powerful than the demonic; and His protection will raise a mighty testimony that can have a "ripple effect" in the spiritual world and impact many for Christ. Satan can threaten all he wants to, but in the end, God wins, every time.

Getting Support for the Supporters

Supporters need support themselves, someone safe they can vent to, ask questions, and help them realize they are not alone in what they are doing. At the very least, every supporter should have a strong church covering, for the spiritual protection this provides, and prayer support for their ministry to survivors. When the going gets tough, the tough ask for prayer support, which can literally "turn the tide" during intense spiritual warfare. Anyone supporting survivors should have their pastor and prayer teams on speed dial on their phones.

Supporters also need spiritually mature mentors they can talk to and get advice about the ups and downs of their ministering to a wounded individual. A mature therapist, prayer team leader, or spiritual parent would be good individuals for this, especially if they also have experience in providing support to traumatized people. Getting a cup of coffee with a mentor, and simply being heard and supported, can go a long way towards preventing burnout. **It is never a good idea to try and support survivors of ritual abuse and mind control "solo"**: at best, the individual burns out, and at worst, may get pulled down or incapacitated spiritually and emotionally. Work with others, and under spiritual authority and accountability; this is a biblical model that is safest.

Another problem with working solo is that the amount of emotional enmeshment that can occur will set the supporter up for sexual seduction. This is more common than most people realize, and can be very damaging for both the supporter and survivor. I have known of marriages broken up and ministries damaged for this very reason.

Chapter 17: Why People Don't Heal

Many, if not all, survivors want to heal. They enter into therapy, begin the hard work, pray, spend their money on therapy and books, journal, join online support groups and "do all the right things." Yet, the survivors struggle. Healing doesn't happen as quickly as they had hoped. Healing is a lot harder than they thought it would be. And some choose to walk away from healing, or stay caught in a perpetual cycle of pain without full healing or integration.

Why is this? Is it lack of desire, or faith, on the part of the survivor? In most cases, no. Then why is it that some people appear not to heal, or to heal very slowly?

There can be many reasons for this apparent lack of progress. In this chapter, I will address some of the major ones, but this is not meant to be comprehensive.

Fear is the number one reason that healing can take so long. This includes the lifelong fear of healing installed with numerous painful setups, in which catastrophic consequences occur if the survivor attempts to break their own programming. This fear can be for the survivor's safety, but most often is for the continued safety of loved ones.

Every survivor of a group that employs modern mind control techniques will have been programmed to protect their closest loves ones, or double binds. Even if they are willing to die to get free, they may not be able to watch those they love die in the process. And these groups will ruthlessly exploit this fear, causing the survivor to attempt to be a "messiah" and "rescue" loved ones by returning to the group, or committing suicide.

Access is the number one cause of a system shutdown, or failure of parts to talk to the survivor who is trying to leave a cult group. As mentioned in the first chapter, this access can include physical access, subliminals, phone texts or messages, videos online, or spiritual access. All it takes is a video (sent by smartphone) of a loved one begging the survivor to save them, or of a torture session with the loved one, for the parts that were formerly working hard in therapy and journaling to stop trying to heal.

Parts may be programmed to believe that they can "never heal" and it is useless to even attempt to do so, in vicious programming loops meant to discourage the survivor. Healing does take time, since the survivor will have numerous parts and years of constant torture, abuse and programming to heal from, with the messages and beliefs embedded in various systems. Working through all the layers and levels can be tiring, and some individuals choose not to pay this price.

A huge cause of failure to heal is the lack of safety and safe support for the survivor. This is the greatest lack of all, since without safety, the survivor will continue to be accessed, reprogrammed and will be unable to dismantle their own programming. If there was more safe, knowledgeable support available for survivors, more survivors would heal. But because most churches lack the knowledge base or willingness to walk with survivors, and offer the emotional support required, many times survivors choose not to take the huge risks associated with healing (the risk of physical torture, or the death of loved ones) in return for weak or nonexistent safety or support.

This is the greatest need for survivors, and the one that is most often unmet. I have prayed for numerous survivors, who have asked me, "Do you know of any safe housing I can go to?" (I do not), or who have asked, "Where do I find safety?" This is a heartbreaking question, and the only response I can give is "Ask God for a miracle; to raise up safety for you where you are, to help you find a safe place to stay." It truly is a miracle when a non-dissociative, non-programmed individual chooses to help survivors. I have known a few in my own life and journey, and they are precious, wonderful and strong people indeed. Not everyone is willing to offer the emotional support, deal with the warfare and provide the prayers that survivors require. But each one that I have known was tremendously blessed by God for what they did.

Some survivors fail to heal because they have a weak walk with God. They may never have had discipleship or support from Christians who can show them the love of God. Their systems may be heavily programmed to reject God, or to embrace a false form of Christianity. I personally believe that only the true God of Christianity can heal a survivor who has lived a lifetime of Occultic abuse and mind control programming. Only He can provide the support, caring and unending love needed, and the forgiveness for what can seem to be an overwhelming amount of evil deeds committed.

I personally believe that we are very close to the "end times" of Revelations, and that the Occultic messiah (or antichrist) is alive. We live in times of great darkness, but also of great revival and breakthroughs. The church is being called to bring revival to the world, and in the process, to help the prisoners break their chains. Satan's army is already in place, awaiting the orders to march. Is the church prepared to help those members of that army that want to break free? The need is much greater than the resources, and this should become a prayer point for every church: to help those fleeing the kingdom of darkness, and its terrible oppression know the love of God and the breakthroughs that Jesus, the true Messiah, can bring.

I have called my ministry Mizpah, or the point of breakthrough and a strong tower for the LORD, for a reason: I want to see churches become part of the breakthrough. Satan is not as powerful as he would like mankind to believe, and I believe the LORD is calling Christians to war. Warfare is not "optional" in these days; to do nothing in these times is to agree with the enemy's agenda.

If you are called to help survivors, pray and get training to do so. If you are not, pray for them and their supporters. Pray that God's will is done on earth, as it is in heaven, and that He will raise up a mighty testimony to His goodness in the lives of the survivors you support or pray for. Heaven is watching, and waiting, to see what the church's response to this need is. My prayer is that you will respond, and become part of what is one of the most wonderful ministries possible: sharing the love of God with wounded souls who have never known what real Christianity looks like. May God bless you for reading this book, and caring for those wounded by Satan's worst blows; and for being part of the healing and restoration process.

About the Author

Since 1999 Svali has written articles and led online groups to help educate survivors and the public regarding dissociation, ritual abuse, mind control and the work of organized occult groups internationally. Her articles and free book (*Breaking the Chain*) have been translated into five languages and read by both survivors and therapists around the world. A former trainer for an international occultic group, she left the group nearly a decade ago, and currently ministers to other survivors through prayer ministry.

You can learn more about Svali and read other articles she has written on her personal blog: svali speaks again. If you are interested in prayer ministry she can be contacted at svalispeaks@gmail.com .

Made in United States
North Haven, CT
14 February 2026

88693418R00057